JOURNEYS TO JUSTICE

JOURNEYS TO JUSTICE

REFLECTIONS ON CANADIAN CHRISTIAN ACTIVISM

JOE GUNN

NOVALIS

Cover design: Martin Gould
Cover image: Citizens for Public Justice
Layout: Audrey Wells

Published by Novalis

Publishing Office
10 Lower Spadina Avenue, Suite 400
Toronto, Ontario, Canada
M5V 2Z2

Head Office
4475 Frontenac Street
Montréal, Québec, Canada
H2H 2S2

www.novalis.ca

Library and Archives Canada Cataloguing in Publication

Gunn, Joe, author
Journeys to justice : Reflections on Canadian Christian Activism/ Joe Gunn.

ISBN 978-2-89688-467-4 (softcover)

1. Social justice--Religious aspects--Christianity. 2. Church and social problems. 3. Christianity and justice. I. Title.

HN31.G86 2018 261.8 C2017-907370-2

Printed in Canada.

We acknowledge the support of the Government of Canada.

5 4 3 2 1 22 21 20 19 18

CONTENTS

ACKNOWLEDGEMENTS

CPJ gratefully acknowledges the Evangelical Lutheran Foundation, ELFEC, for their financial support.

BY MEANS OF AN INTRODUCTION... A LETTER TO NEXT GENERATIONS

Start by doing what's necessary;
then do what's possible;
and suddenly you are doing the impossible.
—attributed to Francis of Assisi

Photo by Jim McIntyre

Dear Benjamin and Daniela,

The inspiration for this book came from an unlikely source – you, Ben!

I remember how, coming home from St. Francis Xavier University in December 2013, you were, like us all, saddened by news of the death of Nelson Mandela. As a Christmas gift, you received a copy of Mandela's autobiography, *Long Walk to Freedom*. As you devoured the book, and shared the stories in it, our family grew in appreciation of Mandela's incredible commitment to racial justice for all South Africans. Newscasts during the holiday season were filled with tributes to this great man, with several stories extolling the anti-apartheid stances of then-Prime Minister Brian Mulroney and External Affairs Minister Joe Clark. Such praise made me increasingly unhappy, as I recalled many of the efforts of Christian churches, union members and solidarity activists who struggled for years to push the reluctant Canadian authorities to impose sanctions, boycott South African goods, deny investments to the apartheid regime, and withdraw the loans of Canadian banks. I found myself needing to tell the stories of how, at your age, we marched and protested, wrote letters, and even how your father delivered his first sermon outlining the Christian case against apartheid in Sunset United Church, Regina, 'way back in February 1979.

And then, in my moment of paternal frustration, I realized that much of this activity took place over a decade before you twins were even present on this Earth! How could I expect millennials to know this history?

Surely, I must take some responsibility for making known the story of the Canadian churches' efforts against apartheid, as well as other epic struggles. How could that history be shared with a new generation? My attempt to share and inspire is in the pages you now hold.

Since you twins have both volunteered at Citizens for Public Justice (CPJ), you know that this ecumenical faith-based organization began operations in the early 1960s. You have heard me say that not a month goes by when I am not approached by a young person who has stumbled for the first time upon our organization's work on poverty eradication, climate justice or refugee rights. They want to know more, and to learn how to get involved – but many also wonder, "How is it that I never heard of CPJ's work before?"

It is entirely possible for your generation of Canadians to grow up in a church community that never shares a sermon about the ecumenical justice endeavours in which their national church participates. Some young people attend various denominational schools, never hearing the words of folks interviewed in this book. Yet, every spring when CPJ opens applications for our annual paid internships, scores of terrific young people (including some of your friends) send in their resumés. The worst part of my job is having to say "no; sorry" to all but one or two of these wonderful young university graduates. There is no doubt in my mind that new activists like you are searching for ways to meld their faith with positive action for social and ecological change. But our institutional structures do not make enough space for your expressions of energy and commitment.

A book such as this is needed for several reasons: because injustice still threatens humanity and all creation; because the exemplary role of others was once inspirational to me and my generation; because the antidote to poor theology is good theology (not the rejection of theology); because the portrayal of religions as conservative societal forces is not the only story. For your dad, engagement in public justice has been the best way to live – and to try to "live out" – the important values that in my generation were passed on by the Christian faith.

I hope your generation can benefit from hearing these stories of struggles that might seem far in the past. You will find it difficult to believe that some of the initiatives described in these interviews were enjoined before the internet existed! The last time a similar project (recounting the story of the ecumenical social justice coalitions) was published was almost 25 years ago, in books like 1994's *Coalitions for Justice*, by Chris Lind and Joe Mihevc, or John Williams' *Canadian Churches and Social Justice*, released a decade earlier. This was well before the various ecumenical social justice coalitions were restructured to form KAIROS in 2001.

HOW DID I PUT THIS BOOK TOGETHER?

I interviewed ten Canadian Christians whom I've known and held as role models in the pursuit of public justice. They often remain unsung heroes, and deserve to be profiled. I wanted to record, in their own words, their anecdotes, their wisdom and the lessons they learned. Restrained by space restrictions for this book, I hope other interviewers might be inspired to include other stories. Since many views on issues exist, and so many people were involved in these movements, I had to do the tough work of choosing only a few issues, and a few interviewees, to give readers a strong sense of what was done, as well as what might be possible today.

In the list of my interview victims, I was keen to include women as well as men, and persons from several faith traditions. It was most difficult to choose figures who were involved in ecumenical movements of national impact from all the regions of Canada, since most ecumenical organizations were headquartered in Toronto. And it was impossible to identify persons to interview from visible minority groups, as these Canadians were not then well represented in positions of church leadership. (Please work to change that.) I chose issues where illustrative struggles were waged, and then attempted to interview key participants who could recount and reflect on these seminal events. In a few cases, I have included concerns addressed by particular Christian churches, believing that their impacts had wider implications for faith-based justice activities.

The wise advice, outrageous humour and long experience of my friend and willing accomplice in so many ecumenical adventures, David Pfrimmer, along with his essay on the theological journey of public ecumenism, were essential to this entire project. His constant encouragement helped frame this work.

To make these perspectives even more relevant to today's public justice advocates, I've gratefully included the reflections of two younger writers, Christine Boyle and Leah Watkiss. Both of these women are inspiring and faithful justice activists who reflect on the work of the previous generation, and then suggest what faith-based social activism must look like today.

Daniela, I was glad that you agreed to get to know better the stories of some of your friends (like Tony Clarke) by transcribing a few interviews. Another blessing was that your aunt, my twin, Mary K., also greatly contributed in the transcribing work – after returning from 35 years living in Chile. You can understand more deeply that the work of solidarity and social change does not only result in anecdotal history. Ben and Daniela, because churches saved thousands of Chilean refugees from torture and death, you now have five Chilean-Canadian cousins. These stories are part of your flesh and blood – and that of thousands of other Canadians.

In April 2017, Angus Reid pollsters reported that a majority of Canadians still say that personal faith and religious beliefs are important in how they think about social issues. So, there should be a strong case for faith communities to develop insightful social analysis, speak out and be heard on the pressing issues of the day, to engage their members in discernment of suitable actions and public advocacy as a result. But your generation doesn't look to the Christian churches for such action today. That's not your fault.

In 1973, when church leaders crossed the country speaking about Ten Days for World Development, there were 220 ecumenical community groups to receive and echo their work. By the 1980s, the Anglican Church of Canada participated in no fewer than 17 ecumenical justice coalitions. In his 2004 book *Radical Compassion: The Life and Times of Archbishop Ted Scott*, author and ecumenical justice activist Hugh McCullum reported that "Those golden days of social justice and activism are gone."

After two decades of working in social justice ministry for the Canadian Conference of Catholic Bishops, Tony Clarke identified, in his 1995 book *Behind the Mitre*, a "moral leadership crisis" among Canada's bishops that was causing them to moderate their progressive leanings and public pronouncements. Bob McKeon, who coordinated the justice office of the Archdiocese of Edmonton, wrote a thesis in 2003 suggesting that the church's progressive leadership after Vatican II had run out of steam by the early 1990s.

In fall 2010, I reported in *The Ecumenist* (Vol. 47, No. 4) on the results of a survey that had been circulated to each of the denominations active in social justice. Most Christian churches continued to cut back on social justice ministries. Over two thirds of the churches had fewer social justice staff than five years earlier; seven of nine churches' justice ministries had suffered budget cuts; and three churches reported greatly decreased effectiveness. A revealing commentary was that "With the sequential decimations of church office staff in all the important member churches of the Canadian Council of Churches, there is nothing like the capacity there used to be to undertake substantial joint work compared to five years ago. We continue to rely on sister organizations for substantial policy work: Project Ploughshares, Citizens for Public Justice, KAIROS." Another similar commentary ended with the words "Unfortunately, those partners are also vulnerable."

A deplorable crisis in Canadian ecumenical justice work occurred more recently. In October 2016, the Catholic bishops announced the end of their participation in KAIROS, Canada's largest faith-based social justice organization. For the first time in a generation, the ecumenical architecture that allowed social justice initiatives to flourish among the major Christian traditions was broken. This defeat for social justice in Canada has deep implications and will be difficult to repair. When the Christian churches deign to speak out on social issues now, political players will know that the leadership of Canada's largest Christian denomination no longer shares the ecumenical consensus. The ability of Christian faith groups to share work, develop common positions and speak together publicly has been dealt a massive blow.[1]

Your generation is painfully aware that Canada's Christian churches have not always served admirably, due to our shadow history of sexual improprieties; Residential School abuses, described as participation in the "cultural genocide" of Indigenous peoples; and hurtful gender inequities and discrimination against LGBTQ persons. The efforts of churches working ecumenically on just causes does not mean that church institutions or personnel have always *been* just. In the words of the recently deceased Fr. Michael Crosby, OFM, a long-time activist in corporate social responsibility, "I have discovered that this call for justice in my own church is usually much harder to proclaim (and even harder to see accepted by its leaders) than any work I have done to bring about greater justice in the corporate and political worlds."

Episcopalian Diana Butler Bass observes in her 2012 book, *The End of Church and the Birth of a New Spiritual Awakening*, that past failures have allowed Christianity to be defined in much public discourse as "mean, bigoted and making people behave badly." Butler Bass also believes that "The history of Christianity can be told as a story of the tension between order and prophecy." At times, this tension seems to describe the struggle for the soul of the churches. Those interested in "order" can spend their time defining "who is in and who is out," easily becoming the voices of judgment and, too often, oppression. Those trying to hear the prophetic voice strive to create a world where, according to Psalm 85:10, "mercy and faithfulness have met, justice and peace have embraced." While the prophetic voice has often been muted, it is always important to hear.

1 Joe Gunn, "A Crowning Highlight of Canadian Ecumenism—Abandoned," *The Ecumenist*, Vol. 54, no. 4 (Fall 2017).

This book is a recounting of how action for justice has transformed our understanding of society, faith traditions, churches, and our role in these institutions. In one interview, I was gently rebuked. "You only remember the glory days," I was told. But the task before us is not the restoration of some gloried past – rather, we seek transformation, a deepening of efforts to reflect God's *shalom* today.

We can't turn back the clock. In Genesis 19:26, Lot's wife was turned into a pillar of salt due to her need to grasp one last glimpse of her past. In every interview, the final question was whether the efforts and achievements of each struggle revealed any lasting lessons that could be relevant today.

In the context of the institutional demise of several denominations, what new structures and engagements are needed if your generation might continue the mission of social solidarity and ecological justice?

Ecumenical justice work needs constantly relevant and shared spiritual foundations. Theology has grown by leaps and bounds during the past generation. In the 1970s, liberation theology emerged in Latin America and served to frame the work of several ecumenical solidarity coalitions. I lived for seven years in that region, and chaired the Inter-Church Committee on Human Rights in Latin America for over a decade, so this tradition's impact on my own beliefs runs deep. Yet, newer expressions broaden our horizons today, resulting in theologies helping to liberate God's people from racial, gender and other oppressions. Advances in scientific knowledge have resulted in eco-theologies based on the new cosmology. The point is that although the gospel does not change, the way we interpret its meaning for justice ministry must always mature and develop.

The Canadian churches are in drastic need of developing new lines of transmission of not only their histories of justice work, but of current action initiatives. No denomination has perfected means of informing the clergy and people in the pews about the biblical basis for justice. Abilities to engage memberships with a view to enhancing ownership and participation in justice initiatives vary tremendously.

The justice work of the future, once ecumenical, will now increasingly be multi-faith. But even this is not enough. To impact change against powerful economic and political forces, faith communities must also reach out to make common cause with citizen movements, research groups and community organizers. Institutions that express a fundamental commitment to the common good will refuse to distance themselves from the means of achieving it. They will become flexible, agile and capable of rapid decision making.

Through the stories of struggle and perseverance in this collection, my hope is that your generation, Ben and Dani, but also any reader, will discover that you have been part of a bigger story. All those petitions you were asked to sign on Sunday mornings and at evening meetings, all those letters you wrote, all those newsletters you shared, allowed you to make a difference.

Please join and directly support independent organizations governed by members, such as Citizens for Public Justice, or groups like KAIROS or Project Ploughshares that have enjoyed institutional church support and governance. As you identify new concerns that need to be addressed, while realizing the limitations of the church institutions that formally organized justice work in this last generation, I hope that you see new opportunities for participation and action for living justly.

It can never be confirmed that Francis of Assisi once offered the advice to "start by doing what's necessary; and then do what's possible." But the stories in this collection show that people of faith have, with God's help, indeed suddenly found themselves "doing the impossible." I know that you and your generation will, too!

Love,
Dad

PART 1

WHERE WE'VE BEEN

THE CHURCHES INFLUENCE REFUGEE POLICIES IN CANADA

Photo by Kevin Sandell

As a representative of the ecumenical work opening the door to Chilean refugees, John Foster (left) was honoured by the Chilean Ambassador to Canada, Alejandro Marisio, in October 2016.

INTERVIEW WITH JOHN FOSTER

Right up into the 20th century, Canadian immigration policy has been decidedly racist. Until the 1970s, Canada had not undertaken a large-scale sponsorship of non-European refugees. In 1974, the Minister of Manpower and Immigration, Robert Andras, released a Green Paper on Canadian immigration policy that caused a stir by referring to the "novel and distinctive features" of persons likely to apply for entry. When the Minister launched public consultations, 50 hearings were held in 21 cities, and churches played a huge lobbying role through a national network called The Inter-Church Project on Population.

During the Cold War era, immigration policy was also charged with ideological considerations. Persons fleeing violence and persecution from right-wing regimes were not easily admitted to Canada. Nonetheless, Canadian churches saved many lives by pressuring the federal government to allow entry of refugees from Chile after the bloody military coup d'état of September 11, 1973.

John Foster tells this amazing story below.

I was a leader in the youth movement of the United Church in the '60s, and a youth representative on the General Council Executive (which is the denomination's chief governing body between biennial conventions). I was doing my Ph.D. at the University of Toronto, and in 1971 I was appointed as a researcher on social issues to the Division of Mission in Canada, where I remained until 1988.

I was interested in Latin America, just because of what was happening in the world. Fighting poverty was a key issue at the World Assembly of Youth (1964), where a leading Brazilian academic addressed us. In 1966, at a national convention in the Laurentians, we formed an International Affairs Working Group for the United Church Young Peoples Union. We were invited to a hemispheric Protestant youth gathering in Puerto Rico, by the regional formation of the World Council of Churches for Latin America. Four Canadians went, met young people from the Dominican Republic, formed continuing bonds and experienced Latin American politics through them. In the mid-'60s, the Dominican dictator Trujillo was overthrown and killed. There were all kinds of revolutionary attempts until in 1965, American marines landed and taught us all a lesson about the military nature of American imperialism.

Similar things were happening among American youth. A conference in Chicago (1966) included Canadian representatives and founded the North American Congress on Latin America (NACLA), which continues today as a research and publishing group. American and Canadian youth began working on the nature of imperialism and exploitation in the hemisphere, in solidarity with Latin American counterparts.

Those were Cold War days. There was official paranoia about communism and the Soviets. In October 1970, Canada experienced the FLQ crisis, and what would now be called domestic terrorism. Civil society organizations and students reacted against the heavy response of the federal government and the RCMP.

While I was beavering away for the United Church, the United Nations convened the third conference on trade and development (UNCTAD, 1972) in Santiago, Chile. Remember that Che Guevara had addressed an earlier conference and challenged the North quite bluntly. Santiago was home to a democratically elected socialist coalition government, led by Salvador Allende. Three church observers went to Santiago: Jerry Hames for the Anglican newspaper; Greg Arbour, a young Catholic law student from Windsor; and me for the United Church.

We were in Chile for at least six weeks. The Canadian official delegation was headed by Paul Martin (senior), Minister of Foreign Affairs. For anyone concerned with international development, debates were seldom boring, and new approaches were being implemented in the society around us. In the halls of the conference, there was not only Catholic commentator Barbara Ward, but people like André Gunder Frank – a leading theorist of dependency theory and a critic of imperialism.

We had time to get out into factories and to the *poblaciones* (shanty towns), and to witness land reform ceremonies where land was being redistributed. The Socialist coalition government involved prominent members of the Catholic left. Political forces outside that government, like the Movement of the Revolutionary Left, were holding marches and demonstrations. The Chilean New Song movement, with artists like Isabel and Angel Parra, Quilapayún, Inti-Illimani and Victor Jara all produced revolutionary folk music and were part of the general excitement of the time.

When the International Affairs Working Group of the United Church's Young Peoples Union became known as the Latin American Working Group (LAWG), Anglican and Presbyterian members joined, as did people from the Student Union for Peace Action. We had a personal connection with Chile when Reverend Arturo Chacon and his partner, Florrie Snow, went back to Chile, in '72 or '73. (This Canadian-Chilean couple was studying in Toronto around 1970. Arturo was a minister in the Methodist church in Chile, and Florrie became the staff member of the Inter-Church Committee on Chile.)

LAWG and their sister group in Toronto, the Development Education Centre, produced a smart little pamphlet called "Chile versus the Corporations." It looked at the role of transnationals trying to upset the Allende government's nationalization of the copper mines. We were planning to take an exposure tour of people to Chile. That plan was interrupted by the coup d'état.

The coup hit us like a lightning bolt. LAWG members, maybe a dozen people, had a little office in the front room of the co-op house where I lived. We swung into high gear, hiring Tim Draimin, a student who had returned from a trip through the hemisphere. We got in touch with the Chacons in Chile and gathered information from sister groups like NACLA in the United States. The World Council of Churches had contacted the Canadian churches to see what their reaction would be to human rights violations, and the coup. After a week or two, the question of political refugees and people seeking asylum became priorities.

Luckily, the leadership of three of Canada's major churches had all visited Latin America within the past few years. That included Archbishop Ted Scott from the Anglican Church, Catholic Bishop William Power, and Rev. Bruce McLeod, Moderator of the United Church. That facilitated the higher priority and quicker response from the denominations.

A week after the coup, two Chilean university students and four Canadians, including Frances Arbour and me, journeyed to Ottawa to see Foreign Affairs officials. (Frances, a former nun who worked in Mexico, later was the executive director of the Inter-Church Committee on Human Rights in Latin America from 1977 to 1985.) We trudged off to the Pearson Building in search of staff responsible for what was happening in Chile. That was a rather frigid encounter. They didn't want to let our six members into the building together, and we were photographed by officials from afar. We felt some paranoia. A Foreign Affairs official assured us that figures about torture and death from Chile were exaggerated, that violence was restricted to the capital city, and that there was nothing to worry about. He did not even acknowledge that a few people (I think at that time about four) had taken refuge in the Canadian Embassy. Apart from them, he stated, all other Chileans would have to apply to come to Canada through normal immigration channels.

At this point in history, Canada had received, on an emergency basis, refugees from Hungary (1956) and Czechoslovakia (1968), and also people of Indian ethic background (1972) from Idi Amin's Uganda. So, there was precedent for Canada to airlift refugees in a special program, even though officially the government was reluctant to admit asylum seekers.

It may be hard to imagine a period when you either came to Canada as an immigrant, or you didn't get in. Refugees from the Soviet Bloc – Cold War allies, so to speak – received special treatment. We were not pleased with the reaction of External Affairs officials. Part of our delegation went off to meet with more sympathetic opposition politicians: people like members of Parliament John Rodriguez and Andrew Brewin from the New Democratic Party (NDP).

A group of us decided to meet weekly at the Canadian Council of Churches, what I called "the Friday afternoon Crisis Club." Council head Rev. Floyd Honey hosted, and staff members Ruth Tillman and Rev. Eoin MacKay contributed. We would monitor and communicate with the Canadian government, passing on appeals from the World Council of Churches and from Latin American churches.

The Canadian Conference of Catholic Bishops got a meeting with the Foreign Minister, Mitchell Sharp, on October 3, 1973, about three weeks after the coup. Fr. Everett McNeil (general secretary of the bishops), Rev. Floyd Honey (general secretary of the Canadian Council of Churches), Dr. Garth Lake and me from the United Church, Fr. Bill Smith from the Missions Office of the Catholic bishops, Ian McKay of the Presbyterians, and the Reverend David Weller from the Anglican Church of Canada gathered.

Mitchell Sharp immediately tried to put us on the defensive by not so subtly suggesting that we were communist sympathizers. Then he said that everything was returning to normal in Chile. (This was not the information we were getting.) We presented a brief that stressed the strongest possible protest against violations of human rights perpetuated by the new regime's bloody seizure of power. Then we requested that Canada immediately receive refugees. That was the beginning of an ongoing effort by a group of Canadian churches and their allies to seek an open door for refugees from Chile.

We stressed that Canada should not recognize the military junta, or give it diplomatic legitimacy. We pointed out that the Allende government was elected in a free, democratic election and overthrown by this military coup. The kind of response we were getting from Sharp suggested a historic stereotype of Latin America, where coups and dictatorships were "normal".

One day later, the government's Canadian Development Corporation gave a five-million-dollar export credit to sell Twin Otter military planes to Chile, and just a couple of days after that, the Canadian government went ahead and recognized the junta.

There was a war for information, and LAWG addressed the media very well. Because we had friends in Chile, and particularly the Canadian-Chilean couple the Chacons, we could get "on the street" reports. Barbara Frum at the CBC radio program "As It Happens" repeatedly linked the home of the Chacons in Chile to Canadian listeners across the country. This was significant, because Florrie and friends reported a continuation of violent incidents by the military that were not being reported by the Canadian Ambassador in Chile or by media who had moved on to the next world crisis.

And when that wasn't enough, we formed the Inter-Church Ad Hoc Committee on Chile, the continuation of the Friday afternoon Crisis Club. Events like Florrie's report of corpses in the Mapocho River in central Santiago led to efforts to send Canadian fact-finders south.

We encouraged the visit to Chile by *Toronto Star* journalist Ian Adams, one of the co-authors of *The Real Poverty Report*, a bestseller in that period. Later on, in the fall, Fr. Bill Smith and another Scarboro Foreign Missionary, Fr. Buddy Smith, both went to Chile to witness what was happening.

There were also visits from Chileans to Canada. Chilean churches organized the ecumenical Committee for Peace, and one of its key members, Lutheran Bishop Helmut Frenz (who was later expelled from Chile), spoke in Canada. Our Ad Hoc Committee on Chile was distributing information to networks across the country, and local solidarity committees were active in various centres across Canada.

At the time of the coup, Canadian Ambassador Ross was in Buenos Aires, Argentina, buying a new car. Embassy staff David

Adam and Marc Dolgin allowed a number of people into the Embassy. By the end of the year, there were close to 50 people in Canadian protection, either in the Embassy downtown or at the Ambassador's home. Ross regarded these folks as the "riff-raff of the Latin American Left." He was resistant to having them, afraid they were going to steal the silver, it seems. Two of the people who were in the Embassy, Marcela and Claudio Duran, now live in Toronto. They were flown out on October 7 along with less than a dozen others. From the churches' point of view, that was insufficient.

The Ambassador's cables were the chief source of first-hand, official information reaching Ottawa. These diplomatic cables were circulated from External Affairs to a number of people in the federal civil service, including Bob Thompson, who was working at the Canadian International Development Agency. Bob had copies of these cables passed on to the Opposition politicians, and ultimately to the press. On November 5, NDP member of Parliament John Harney read the cables into the record of Parliament and confronted Mitchell Sharp yet again with Canada's failure to respond. (The government set out to find the whistle-blower and force his resignation. That's a whole other story in itself....)

With that revelation of the government's misinformation, the Foreign Affairs Department sent a special mission to Chile. Geoff Pearson, the son of former Prime Minister Lester Pearson, went on that mission. I'm told that he returned from Chile and went directly into a Cabinet meeting, which was one of the key moments when the government's policy shifted.

Around the same time, Allende's widow, Hortensia, addressed a big crowd at Convocation Hall in Toronto. She met with the churches and with Prime Minister Pierre Trudeau. The government was also under pressure from the UN High Commission for Refugees. On November 26, the Cabinet Committee on Social Policy decided that some 300 to 1,000 refugees could be accepted under reduced criteria than for regular immigrants. Some government support for resettlement, transportation and accommodation, language training, job placement, winter clothing and other necessities would be provided. That was called Special Movement Chile.

On December 3, we met again with Mitchell Sharp and with Immigration Minister Robert Andras and pushed them to move swiftly. Simple things like finding seats on airplanes were leading to further delays. Ottawa sent an RCMP officer to the Embassy in Santiago to facilitate security checks. In the first part of "Special Movement Chile," 137 people came to Toronto in January, months after we had begun the pressure.

The government argued that no Chileans wanted to come to Canada. Every excuse you can think of was used. However, as of January 18, I've got a record of 3,100 applications. By February 3, there were 9,300. Of those, between 100 and 500 were non-Chileans resident in Chile, under the UN's protection. About 400 of those ultimately got in through that special program.

It didn't all just end in the early part of '74. We were aware that more people needed and wanted to come. The Chilean dictatorship also wanted to get rid of political detainees in its prisons. Here was an odd coincidence of interests: the Canadian churches were interested in getting those people out of prison, and General Pinochet was anxious to dispose of his compulsory guests. George Cram from the Anglican Church took leadership in developing a proposal that reassured the government's fear about accepting revolutionaries from Latin America, while providing assurances that people really wanted to come to Canada.

Cram, Buddy Smith and François Lapièrre (who later was appointed bishop of St. Hyacinthe) went together to Chile to consult with the Embassy and set up criteria to prioritize those who really needed to come to Canada. They were leaving prison, but they and their families might never return to their country. Those who had been tortured were highest on the list. Cram, Smith and Lapierre gained access to the prisons where these people were held, did interviews, and got agreement from individuals and their families and, ultimately, the Canadian officials. Cram testifies that some who were given the option of coming said, "Oh, no. There are other people who have a much more urgent case than us," and stepped back, exhibiting incredible human solidarity.

Ultimately, the success of that first tranche was such that the churches put together a proposal for another hundred. This is something that had not been done before in Canadian experience. It was a remarkable and original approach, one that might serve in other situations today.

Many lives were saved. There are various estimates – at least 9,000 and maybe 20,000 people came to Canada, in a variety of ways. One of the people who came on the first plane to Toronto talked about how, on the bus to the Santiago airport, people shook their fists and threw things at the vehicle because they were escaping from the military dictatorship.

This work was pioneering Canadian ecumenism. Leading Anglicans, Lutherans, Quakers, Catholics, people from the Catholic religious orders, United and Presbyterians collaborated. We created a Canadian Fund for Refugees from Chile.

We deeply appreciated the role of church partners inside Chile who took personal risks to direct people in need to get to Canada. One group of progressive Brazilians, escaping a military dictatorship at home, had taken residence in Allende's Chile, but fled for temporary refuge in Panama after the coup. The Panamanian government wasn't particularly welcoming, but in February 1974, the network of churches notified us that these people were coming through Jamaica and must not be turned back. (Today you wouldn't be able to get on a plane in Jamaica unless you had a visa to get into Canada.) A group of us met them at customs in Toronto and welcomed them to Canada. Some of the leading members of the group were Herbert da Sousa and his wife, María. Herbert found an intellectual home at York University, and within a very few years helped establish the Centre of Latin American and Caribbean Studies, one of Canada's main academic centres on Latin America.

After "the Friday afternoon Crisis Club" became the Inter-Church Ad Hoc Committee on Chile, and refugees began to arrive, South Americans in Canada came to the churches and argued that other military dictatorships were in cahoots with each other, all trained by the United States.

So, in 1976, the Inter-Church Committee facilitated an inter-party parliamentary investigatory team that included Andrew Brewin (NDP), Louis Duclos (Liberal) and David MacDonald, who was then a Conservative. A trip was planned to visit Chile, Uruguay and Argentina. Frances Arbour and George Cram did some preliminary investigation to see which groups could receive the MPs. In several cases, they tried to talk to people who were underground, trying to keep out of the hands of the military. Extreme security precautions were taken in this remarkable enterprise. But they found allies like Argentinian Adolfo Perez Esquivel, who became a very prominent international human rights advocate and won the Nobel Peace Prize. On the day the MPs attempted to get into Chile, the junta denied them entry.

The trip resulted in a 1976 joint report called "One Gigantic Prison." It denounced Canada's slow acceptance of the almost 20,000 persons needing to flee Argentina, taking about six months to process them and judging eligibility more on the point system and manpower needs than on their grave personal situation.

That report became the basis for remandating what became the Inter-Church Committee on Human Rights in Latin America (ICCHRLA) in 1976. ICCHRLA ultimately became a part of KAIROS. The work of its staff and members in carefully documenting human rights violations in South and Central America was used to continuously pressure the Canadian government at home and at the United Nations. The late Rev. Charles Harper, a Presbyterian minister at the World Council of Churches' office for human rights in Latin America, worked with us to give their testimony international profile. The famous Mothers of the May Square from Buenos Aires, similar groups from Uruguay, and various groups who were working on human rights and refugee facilitation in Chile were brought to the UN Commission on Human Rights in Geneva.

The churches pursued refugee issues with considerable energy and created an inter-church refugee group in the late 1970s. Kathleen Ptolemy, and then Tom Clark, staffed what became by the 1980s the Inter-Church Committee on Refugees.

The response to the Chilean refugees by congregations across the country at the community level was admirable. This is one of the considerable strands in the weave of Canada's reputation as a sympathetic country, a hospitable country, towards refugees. Today, confronted by refugees freezing their way across the border near Emerson, Manitoba, Canadians have again responded. This testifies to a certain kind of warmth and hospitality to people in need.

Many of the refugees from the fall of the Socialist government in Chile were leftists, and not largely church people. It was a surprise to many that they were received by congregations across the country, helping them get language training, clothing or whatever they needed.

The focus on assisting Latin American refugees and testifying about human rights in the hemisphere brought Canadian churches and their personnel into practical alliances with similar groups in Latin America. Reflecting on the experience facilitated theological development, as "liberation theologies" blossomed in the '70s and '80s.

Five to 10 years later, the churches and church networks got heavily involved around the Central American wars and the Nicaraguan revolution, which triumphed in 1979. Before the Chileans came to Canada, the number of Latin Americans in Canada and the priority of Latin America in Canadian foreign policy were low. Eastern Europe was much more prominent; perhaps even Africa as a development objective was more prominent. I hypothesize that the Central American solidarity movement became one of the most powerful forces that the Canadian government had to deal with, because Canadians had met, and had learned from, these Chilean refugees who were now dispersed among Canadian communities.

John Foster was raised and educated in Saskatchewan, beginning in a one-room stone rural public school and concluding with an honorary Doctor of Divinity from St. Andrew's College, Saskatoon. He was national chief executive officer for OXFAM-Canada, was a researcher at the North-South Institute, has taught at several universities, and is a father, grandfather and partner. John has been chair of the Social Watch alliance of organizations in more than 60 countries and vice-chair of the Commonwealth Civil Society Advisory Committee. He is a committed member of the Ottawa Gay Men's Chorus, which performed one of his original works on its 30th anniversary in 2017.

CANADIAN CHURCHES NEGOTIATE THE PRIVATE SPONSORSHIP OF REFUGEES

Photo by Philip Janzen

INTERVIEW WITH BILL JANZEN

Today, we take for granted that many church congregations are intimately involved in the reception and settlement of refugees. In recent years, the generous response to Syrian refugees has been particularly noteworthy. Canada is one of the very few countries on the planet that allows for the private sponsorship of these brothers and sisters in need. But that was not always the case.

By 1975, the defeat of the US military in Vietnam seemed inevitable; Vietnam invaded Cambodia in 1978. Over 700,000 "boat people" fled Indochina throughout these years in perilous attempts to escape the violence.

Canadians wanted to respond, but in previous crises, like the Chilean coup of September 1973, protest and pressure on government was all that could be done.

With 1978's new immigration law, however, small groups of five persons willing to sponsor could receive and settle refugees. But they could also be exposed to substantial financial liabilities during this first year of their commitment.

It was in this context that the first formal agreement to privately sponsor refugees was signed between churches and the federal government. The Mennonite Master Agreement of March 5, 1979, was followed by agreements with the Presbyterian Church of Canada (March 9) and the Christian Reformed Churches of Canada (April 5). By the end of August, 28 national church organizations and Catholic or Anglican dioceses had signed master agreements. By March 1981, the total had reached 47.

Bill Janzen tells us in his own words what led to this historic first agreement.

I started working in 1975 as the director of the Ottawa office of the Mennonite Central Committee (MCC) Canada. What exactly were my duties? Well, I kept wondering about that for the next 34 years! But broadly speaking, I was to help with the governmental aspects of MCC's work, whether national or international. Refugee policy and settlement issues were always part of my brief.

The government signed on to the (1951) UN Convention on Refugees only in June 1969. It hesitated because by committing to that, the government was surrendering a bit of sovereignty. By accepting the Convention, they were giving rights to people who might come to Canada's doorstep.

In the 1970s, the government set up the Refugee Status Advisory Committee, to advise the Minister when a person came to Canada and claimed refugee status. The Committee reviewed their application and then made a recommendation.

Until the end of the '70s, there were never more than 300 refugees accepted in a year. It was pretty small stuff.

There was also an Immigration Appeal Board, which was not strictly about refugees but had some humanitarian powers. So, if anybody came to Canada and was issued a deportation order, that order could be appealed to the Immigration Appeal Board. The Board had the authority to use some humanitarian powers in deciding whether to set aside that deportation order. On the face of it, that had nothing to do with refugees, but in reality, some of the applicants may have been refugees. If one goes back to the 1920s, after the First World War, there were about 21,000 Mennonites who fled from the newly formed Soviet Union and made it to Canada. Technically, they were not refugees, but for all practical purposes they were. A refugee didn't have a clear legal standing until much more recently.

After 1956, there were 37,000 Hungarians who made their way to Canada. I believe they were not technically called refugees, but a number of them were Jewish people. The Jewish community became active in hosting and welcoming them. Also, since a majority was Catholic, Hungarian Catholics opened their homes generously. With the people from Vietnam, there wasn't quite that kind of a constituency to lobby for the entry of the boat people. There wasn't already a large network of people of Indochinese nationality in Canada (as opposed to several of the previous groups that had arrived from Europe).

However, the Mennonite Central Committee had been active in Vietnam since 1954 doing all kinds of relief work. The French were defeated in 1954, but then gradually the American war built up and so there were people fleeing the violence. The MCC had done resettlement work in South Vietnam, helping with village development projects. The Canadian Mennonite Central Committee and the American Mennonite Central Committee always did their international work together, and the American Committee was very critical of American involvement in Vietnam. So a strong debate in Mennonite churches in Canada and the United States developed. Should MCC be more critical of Western governments supporting the government in the South, and against the communist North?

The fact that MCC had a program in Vietnam and that the debate had long been in the minds of Mennonite churches created a certain amount of sympathy towards the refugees. Canadian Mennonites (much more so than American Mennonites) included a sizable portion who had fled the communist government in Russia. So, after 1975, when the communist North took over the South, there was sympathy for Vietnamese who were fleeing the victorious communists. When the boat people were in the news in the fall of 1978, it became the big story and developed a responsive constituency in the Mennonite world.

People fled Vietnam on the high seas. Many of them lost their lives. Many were exploited by ship owners and dumped on the shores of Thailand and Malaysia. That struck a deep chord among Mennonites. At MCC's annual meeting in January 1979, I was told to go back to Ottawa and try to work out a simple arrangement so that our churches could bring over refugees.

In April 1978, a new Immigration Act had come into force. One small provision in that Act was that any five Canadians could sponsor a refugee if they would then assume full responsibility for that refugee for at least one year. Unfortunately, this assumed liability created a barrier because people began to imagine worst-case scenarios for liability.

Back in Ottawa, I had some fairly high-level contacts in the Immigration department, including Kyle Best, the Assistant Deputy Minister. So I phoned him to set up a meeting. Several of my colleagues from the MCC office in Winnipeg came, and we met with Best and several officials. We sketched out the broad outlines of an 11-page agreement. In a way, it was very simple. The basic principle was that MCC as a national organization would assume liability, and then the individual Mennonite churches (or other churches that might want to come under our auspices) would do the actual work of receiving the refugees. If there were liability issues, they would fall back on the national organization.

After that meeting, Gordon Barnet and I were given the task of writing up the agreement. We met I don't know how many times over the next several weeks, always checking with our respective colleagues. Very soon we had a draft agreement that we thought was workable. MCC's Board approved it at a special meeting. On March 5, there was a little ceremony in Winnipeg where (Liberal) Minister of Immigration Bud Cullen and our executive director signed it. Joe Clark's Conservatives won the election in May of that year, but this agreement was done under the Liberals.

In the agreement, we talked quite a bit about the flow of communications. For example, if the Mennonite church in rural Saskatchewan where I grew up got a letter of authorization from the MCC, then that church would go to an immigration officer in Saskatoon and that immigration office would then move forward. That office would not ask any further questions about whether this little Mennonite church had the capital or wherewithal to carry through with their commitment. It made things a lot easier for the Immigration department. They didn't have to do any vetting of any of the groups that came forward. They would then communicate with the embassy in Bangkok and they'd select a family of refugees and pretty soon they would be on their way. There would have to be some medical tests, but it would move very quickly. In that agreement, there was also a provision for certain (difficult) joint assistance cases, where there might be some special needs. The government would provide some extra resources for groups who carried that responsibility.

So it was a remarkable thing.

A new book by former Immigration officials Michael Molloy, Peter Duschinsky, Kurt Jensen and Robert Shalka, called *Running on Empty: Canada and the Indochinese Refugees, 1975–1980,* quotes Gordon Barnet, after he came back from meetings with me, saying that he had returned to his officials and told them, "Look, you told me to squeeze out as much from the church groups as possible and make the government liable for as little as possible. I don't really want to do it that way. I like the way the Mennonites are negotiating and I think we should be a little more forthcoming." The Joint Assistance Programming partly came out of that. I didn't know it at the time. That was a nice thing.

Very soon, other churches signed virtually identical agreements. The man with whom we were negotiating had some personal ties with the Catholic bishop of Pembroke, and he persuaded that bishop to talk with other bishops, so a lot of Catholics quickly came on board.

There is one thing I should say with regards to the United Church and Anglican Church, particularly. They had a more difficult experience negotiating with the Canadian government because there were some hard feelings among officials. The churches had really gone to bat for refugees who had come from Chile when Pinochet took over in September 1973. The government of Canada had dug in its heels and did not want to take very many of them. I think they originally offered to take a thousand, perhaps, so not a large number, and so those larger churches felt that the government had an unfulfilled responsibility.

There was some criticism that MCC was helping the government to offload some of its responsibility. I think, in retrospect, that we were maybe a little bit naive, because at that point we were not as fully involved in ecumenical work as we later became. So we just moved forward. And I think one can be a little self-critical and say, "Well, the US had been such a huge player in that war and the whole anti-communist agenda was strong, so helping people flee a communist regime was in a sense fortifying that view." One could make some criticisms of the initial agreement in that way. On the other hand, there were other dynamics in play, because in Vietnam, there was a certain amount of anti-Chinese ethnic cleansing. In Cambodia, there was likewise an anti-Vietnamese ethnic cleansing. There were all kinds of dynamics going on in that part of the world. One could justify immediately helping these fleeing people on many grounds...

It was remarkably healthy that we had the American Mennonites to debate with. Mennonites had a history of fleeing communism in both the Canadian and the American experience. But American Mennonites had a decade of hard criticism of the American government for fighting the war. How we worked with those two realities was an enriching challenge.

Also, there was an effort during the war to send some relief to the North to demonstrate that we were not totally tied to the political agenda in the South, even though most of our work was in the South.

Here I'd like to tell a story that hasn't yet been told...

At first, the Liberal government was going to bring in some 5,000 refugees (which at that time seemed like a pretty high number). Then, after Joe Clark's government won, and Flora MacDonald was the Minister of Foreign Affairs, they raised that number to 8,000. But then something else happened...

My MCC colleague John Wheeler from Winnipeg was active in bringing in refugees, among over 300 Canadian Mennonite congregations bringing in refugees from Southeast Asia. Wheeler was sent over there to see what was happening on the ground and to find out whether there was a need for more workers to help in the selection process. Anyway, in the July 16, 1979, issue of *Maclean's* magazine, there's a nice picture and interview of Wheeler among refugees and Wheeler says, “Why doesn’t Canada raise the number to 50,000?”

On July 20-21, Flora MacDonald was in Geneva and said, “Canada is taking 50,000 refugees.” I talked with (government official) Mike Molloy and asked if he knew of any other place where that number 50,000 was mentioned. Molloy assured me it could not have come from within the government, as the Department was not of that mindset at all. Molloy said he had no doubt that Flora MacDonald (or someone in her office) saw that *Maclean’s* article and said, “We can go with this; it will catch the public imagination.”

In the end, Canada welcomed 60,000 Indochinese refugees, with over 6,000 being sponsored by Mennonites. When the idea of granting the Nansen Medal (granted by the UN High Commissioner for Refugees in recognition of outstanding service to the cause of refugees and displaced people) was first raised, apparently there were some in the Immigration department who said, “It should be given to the MCC.” Others were convinced that no, it should be given to the churches. I don’t know the details about whether those discussions really happened, but I heard of them, and, quite appropriately, in 1986 the Medal was presented to “the people of Canada.”

Does the private sponsorship of refugees absolve government of its primary responsibility in bringing refugees to Canada? Well, I’m not sure…

You want the government at the very least to set criteria that are fair. And in this situation, the 1978 Immigration Act defined a refugee by the 1951 UN Convention, but also provided for a “designated class.” The government named Southeast Asians a “designated class,” so they became by definition refugees. That capacity to create a designated class removed a huge obstacle to letting people come in. The question is “On what basis does a government use that power to declare that this bunch of people is a designated class?” Even if the government were to do nothing else, we would like it to be fair in this matter. Those who flee a communist regime shouldn't be given preferential treatment at the expense of those who flee a different problem. That's a very basic element.

Of course, I do believe that private sponsorship is a healthy thing for us as a society. I've always thought that once people do this and have a hands-on experience, it kind of enlivens their sense of citizenship. People begin to think, "I can have a voice in what's happening in my society. I'm a player." I'm sympathetic to experiences that engender that kind of feeling.

I do have a huge respect for every group, large or small, who works at refugee sponsorship. I've been directly involved with two families, and helping some little kid get registered for soccer is great. You know his dad was killed in Africa, and getting him out to soccer practice or registered for summer camp or helping them with summer tutoring when they have difficulty in school, it all requires a lot of legwork. People who are willing to do this are wonderful. There just is no substitute for that. If nobody does it, newcomers become vulnerable in this society to all kinds of negative things.

Obviously, the government itself has a very major responsibility to also bring in people who are fleeing for their lives.

Service and advocacy can supplement each other. I remember in 1987, the government was bringing in legislation affecting people from Latin America making their way to the Canadian border through the United States. I remember coming before a parliamentary committee and describing what we were doing to help people from Central America. MCC had people in Texas, and good contacts with the Canadian consulate in Dallas and several other places in the States. We could get people to Canada. Because we were able to describe very hands-on work, the MPs became remarkably sympathetic. Dan Heap was an NDP MP on the committee at that time. Dan wrote me a letter (I still have it) saying, "Bill, until you came this one Conservative Member of Parliament was the most opposed to anything that could be raised. But when you told your stories about actual people, since then he's been totally different. Whatever happened, it communicated with him." So sometimes the fact of having hands-on work can provide a wonderful basis upon which to do advocacy.

There's another dimension, however. In the last several years, I've been at three major events to mark the boat people coming here. They're all great, but they play up what Canada did. And what we try to do at MCC is remind people we'd been involved in Vietnam since 1954, and continued to be involved even after the South Vietnamese government fell and the new communist government wouldn't let us have personnel stationed there. Vietnam, because of its geography, is so vulnerable to typhoons and floods. So we sent relief shipments and we also sent tools for demining farmers' fields so they wouldn't step on land mines. Then we sent delegations to see what was being well used. In the late 1970s here in Ottawa, I met with people a number of times to arrange those visits. But at those big events here we "boast" about how good we were in bringing refugees to Canada. There is almost total silence about the fact that "Hey, there was a whole bunch of people that stayed there [Vietnam] and had a very hard time. What did we do for them?"

It's a little bit shallow that that side of the story has gotten so little attention. In the long run, the solutions to the problems of the world aren't going to be solved by bringing refugees to resettlement countries. As much as I support refugee resettlement, we must find other ways of resolving these problems.

I was in Vietnam in 1986, and it was an oppressive place. Saigon was now called Ho Chi Min City. You could talk to a few people about earlier years when American involvement had been so high, but they were very tight-lipped. They would not speak up. I remember we met with the Catholic bishop in that city who was well aware that the Vietnamese government officials bringing the delegation were watching him very, very closely.

One must acknowledge that quite a few people who were able to get on boats were those who had resources to pay to get to Thailand and Malaysia. I daresay that in quite a few instances, we were not dealing with the poorest of the poor. So yes, private sponsorship was a great thing and I'm deeply grateful. I think that the Vietnamese have made an incredible contribution to Canada. But it's not all black and white. At times, you live with realities where you do good, but there is somewhat of a shadow to that good, as well.

It was the right thing to do, but let me draw a little parallel that illustrates this conundrum. Years ago, Romeo Maione was the director of the NGO division in the Canadian International Development Agency (CIDA). Great man, deeply rooted in Catholic social thought. I remember him saying that the money that the government gives to NGOs is fairly small (considering the whole CIDA budget). And he said that when the decisions are made around that Cabinet table, there's a bit of a temptation to say, "Okay, we'll allocate a couple hundred million for the NGOs and then the NGOs will be busy. They'll be working energetically on their projects in different parts of the world, and that will provide popular support for what we do with the rest of the CIDA money. It will shield criticism of what we do. We can do political things with the rest of the CIDA money, some of which should really not be classified as aid at all."

Romeo was aware that he was being cynical. He certainly believed in the NGO work, there was no doubt about that, but he wanted us to be aware that in the larger game of things, NGOs could be perceived that way.

I felt a little bit that way with refugee work, too, that government can keep small groups busy doing sponsorship and holding celebratory events about the good things we've done.

I think one must always, especially for churches, try to keep a genuine critical eye, a serious analysis, on what's happening in the broader picture of Canadian foreign policy or the broader world. There are hundreds of thousands of people in refugee camps in Africa right now, where there is very little movement, and they're certainly not in the headlines. What are we doing about that?

Bill Janzen grew up in Saskatchewan, served a 30-month term with the Mennonite Central Committee in the Congo, and went to university in Winnipeg. He holds a Ph.D. in Political Science from Carleton University, and another M.A. in Religious Studies from the University of Ottawa. He has published several books and articles and has served as a part-time minister.

Bill was the first director of the Mennonite Central Committee's Ottawa office, from 1975 to 2008, serving on various ecumenical coalitions. From 1993 to 1995, Bill, his wife, Marlene, and their two children lived in Cairo.

PROJECT NORTH DEFENDS INDIGENOUS RIGHTS – THE MACKENZIE VALLEY PIPELINE PROPOSAL

Photo by Matthew Kunkel

INTERVIEW WITH JOHN A. OLTHUIS

Canada was 107 years old when the biggest project in the nation's history to date was proposed: a $10 billion pipeline to bring frontier supplies of gas 4,000 kilometres south to Canada and export markets in the United States. Several consortia of some of the world's largest private companies, and even a "Canadian" variant, spent hundreds of millions of dollars to win the prize of building their version of the high-pressure gas line. Only thus, Canadians were told, would we be able to avoid "freezing in the dark."

But the Dene Nation, along with many faith communities, said "no." Instead, they called for a 10-year moratorium on such development until Aboriginal land claims were settled, environmental protection guaranteed, and proof provided that the pipelines were really needed and would be of benefit to all.

In 1975, Canadian Christian churches launched Project North, a coalition designed to defend Aboriginal rights, promote just land claims, and thus change the historic relationship between Aboriginal people and Canadians. On Labour Day, the Catholic bishops released a pastoral letter questioning the pipeline projects, called "Northern Development: At What Cost?"

After the federal government appointed Judge Thomas Berger to lead the Mackenzie Valley Pipeline Inquiry, he held 18 months of hearings throughout the North, and in May/June 1976, travelled across southern Canada. More than 400 people spoke, creating an event "more like an inquiry into the future of a great nation and its people."

John Olthuis was a leader in the opposition to the Mackenzie Valley pipeline proposals. Here he describes some of the struggle that resulted in that project never being built.

I grew up in Edmonton as part of a rather typical, albeit somewhat conservative, Christian family – except that my father let it be known that loving your neighbour was an important part of the gospel message. I studied law in the early 1960s because I naively thought law was a way to work for justice. In my early years of practice, I discovered (it was a bit of a shock) that to a large extent, the legal system was set up to protect vested interests and capitalism without more than an occasional passing thought to the disadvantaged and marginalized.

In my search for a better place to work for justice, I eventually became research director for what was then somewhat inaptly called The Committee for Justice and Liberty Foundation

(CJL). (Formed in 1963, CJL was a precursor of Citizens for Public Justice.) Citizens for Public Justice (CPJ) is a much more appropriate name.

CJL's desire to speak to public issues from a Christian platform attracted me. I started looking at the implications of the proposal of seven of the world's largest energy companies (the seven sisters) to build the Mackenzie Valley pipeline to carry natural gas from the Canadian Arctic down through the Northwest Territories and Alberta into the US. I suggested, and the CJL Board agreed, that it would be a good idea for CJL to develop a "Just Energy Policy for Canada" as a measuring stick to address the pipeline proposals.

At the time, the seven sisters and their kin (rather than governments) both made and implemented energy policy. In the case of the Mackenzie Valley pipeline, the federal government, based on nothing other than that the "seven sisters" wanted to build it, decided that it should be built. The next step was the National Energy Board (NEB) hearings. These were basically a rubber-stamping process to grant the energy proponent what is ironically called a "Certificate of Public Convenience and Necessity." (What Public? Whose Convenience? and What Necessity?) The NEB decision-making framework and its record of decision making demonstrated that a project would inevitably be approved if it was economically feasible. You could ask the NEB: What about the environment? What about Aboriginal rights? What about overconsumption of energy? They would answer, "We do need to minimize the impacts to the extent possible, but we do that in the conditions that we attach to our pipeline approvals." With that framework, impacts, no matter how severe, could never lead to a project being rejected. Impacts were afterthoughts and never part of the decision making.

The CJL Just Energy Policy called for energy decisions to be made after taking a variety of factors into account, particularly the impact on marginalized people and the environment. At the time, the US was consuming 40 percent of the world's energy with 6 percent of global population. Between Canada and the US, we were about 8 percent of the world's population and were using almost 50 percent of the world's energy. So why build another massive pipeline? It was designed primarily to export gas to the US; to feed their massive appetite for energy and to feed the avarice of some of the world's largest multinational companies. The negative impacts would be on the Dene Aboriginal people and on their environment. So CJL and the Dene Nation (whom I also represented at the hearings) became intervenors in the NEB Mackenzie Valley hearings.

This was at a time when the Club of Rome was expressing grave concern about the carrying capacity of the environment. E.F. Schumacher's *Small Is Beautiful* was being read, and Barry Commoner's *Poverty of Power* convincingly argued that the whole system was in reverse. Commoner said it should be the other way around: the ecosystem should be first, and then the production system should be based upon that capacity, and conservation considerations and the economic production system should reflect those realities. CJL proposed a different approach and advocated a Just Energy Policy that reflected a different set of values and objectives.

Today, looking back at those eight objectives through a 40-year lens, I find they are still relevant. They are listed in the 1977 book I wrote with Hugh and Karmel McCullum, *Moratorium: Justice, Energy, the North, and the Native People.*

Strategically, we decided that rather than saying that the pipeline should never be built, we would call for a moratorium on the construction with the hope that such would engender public discussion about energy policy: its goals, its impacts and a different decision-making framework.

We first proposed the moratorium to the Standing Committee on Natural Resources of the House of Commons in February 1976. They had heard a lot from the oil and gas industry lobby about the need for this pipeline, even though the natural gas was primarily destined for the US. Joe Greene, Canada's Minister of Energy, Mines and Resources, had said that Canada had 372 years of natural gas left. But all of a sudden, a few years later, hocus-pocus, the message coming from Ottawa was that Canada was running out of natural gas! The numbers didn't make sense because they were based on different price projections. Lower-price scenarios showed fewer proven resources, and higher-price scenarios showed higher proven reserves. (Some reserves are costlier to bring to market than others.) So with expert advice we showed how the oil and gas industry misused numbers to make their case for more pipelines, when in fact current supplies were more than adequate.

I remember my first discussions with Dene Nation representatives after CJL reached out to them. We said, we know you don't need our help, but we would like to walk alongside you in your quest to create the public space you need to exercise your right to self-determine your society. We explained that we would like to participate in the public debate, based on CJL's Just Energy Policy, and call for a moratorium on the construction of any pipeline until the Dene Nation had reached a Comprehensive Land Claims Agreement with Canada. A provision of that Agreement would be that Dene Nation consent would be required for all projects on or through Dene land. Dene Nation leader George Erasmus responded by saying that the Dene would welcome any attempt to change Canadian values. The Dene were feeling the pipeline pressure because of the consumer values of Canadian society, values that did not respect the Dene or their environment.

And so we began preparation work to cross-examine the panels of witnesses presented by the Arctic Gas Consortium at the NEB hearings. We prepared CJL expert witness panels to support CJL's proposed Just Energy Policy and a moratorium.

It became clear that Marshall Crowe, the NEB chair, should not have been appointed to chair the panel mandated to decide on the pipeline application, as he participated in putting the Arctic Gas Proposal together. So, with the support of other intervenors, CJL took the matter to court, based on the argument that Crowe's work with the pipeline consortium raised a reasonable apprehension that he would be biased in favour of the Arctic Gas pipeline application.

The Federal Court of Appeal concluded there was no apprehension of bias, but on appeal the Supreme Court of Canada said there *was* an apprehension of bias, and Crowe was removed as chair of the hearings. After some delay, the hearings were restarted with a new chair. That put CJL on the national map. At the NEB hearings and around the court proceedings, we at first took a lot of "David versus Goliath" kidding and some derision from the oil and gas company folks, but that turned to anger when we won the case.

The Supreme Court decision was a shocking outcome for Ottawa politicians, bureaucrats and the oil and gas lobby. They were used to playing musical chairs with one another.

In the end, that decision proved fatal for the Mackenzie Valley proposal. The delay caused by the need to restart the NEB hearings with a new chair was crucial. Mr. Justice Berger tabled his report calling for a moratorium on that pipeline in June 1977, while the hearings were under way, effectively killing the Arctic Gas Proposal. The NEB then had no choice and ruled against Arctic Gas, but approved the Foothills Alaska Highway pipeline. That project never did get built either, at least in part because of the public awareness of the impacts on the rights and traditional activities of Aboriginal Nations and the environmental impacts raised in the NEB hearings – and, more particularly, the Berger Commission's southern public hearings.

The CJL panels of witnesses included The Most Reverend Ted Scott, Primate of the Anglican Church of Canada, and Bishop Remi De Roo, from the Canadian Conference of Catholic Bishops. For the first time, a regulatory board such as the NEB heard the testimony of church leaders who spoke to the human and environmental impact of large energy projects. I will never forget the impression made when Primate Scott arrived in his full regalia to give evidence. The NEB heard that not all Christians endorsed unfettered economic growth and careless capitalism.

We also called University of Toronto economists Mel Watkins and Abraham Rotstein, international development researcher Donald Simpson and University of Toronto political scientist Peter Russell as expert witnesses to speak to a broader array of social, economic, constitutional and public interest matters that should be considered when making decisions on massive energy projects.

The case that CJL presented through its panels of witnesses and in argument on behalf of its members and the Dene Nation focused to a large extent on the need for a new decision-making framework that considered project impacts on matters such as the rights of Aboriginal peoples and the environment in the decision about whether a project should or should not be approved. In the economically focused decision-making framework of the time, a framework that sadly is still the predominant framework today, impacts, no matter how severe, do not lead to project denial.

Protest and prophecy are both powerful. Today, efforts need to continue, with urgency, in all ways, to change the decision-making framework. Unless law-making objectives change in Parliament and the Legislatures, and unless the decision-making framework for regulatory boards and agencies changes, we are always going to get the same unbridled economic-growth-first outcome. And justice-minded folks will continue to end up fighting to minimize damages, rather than participating in a holistic decision-making process that questions whether massive projects like pipelines should be built.

In preparation for the May/June 1976 southern hearings of the Berger Commission, CJL did a lot of work with the church coalitions, particularly with Project North. Peter Hamel of the Anglican Church wrote in *Coalitions for Justice* (1994) that 20 percent of the over 450 briefs presented to Berger in the southern hearings were given by church-based groups. Those were the days when it was possible to call Primate Scott directly and ask him to come to Ottawa for a press conference and he would be there the next day. His comments would receive wide press coverage.

In the end, 183 groups supported CJL's call for a moratorium – from Marxists to groups focused on local economies. At the NEB hearings, I had interesting elevator and corridor conversations with oil and gas company lawyers – they in their fancy suits and I, more often than not, in my work boots and plaid shirt. They called CJL and others "special interest groups." They ironically referred to themselves as "public interest representatives." Many of the discussions focused on what constitutes the public interest. Who decides? Does the concept change over time?

Project North's staff and southern support network were key to the success of the Berger Commission southern hearings. There were Project North Dene support groups in many places across the country, from Saint John's to Victoria. NDP leader Tommy Douglas was also very supportive. CJL met with him, and on one occasion he bought several hundred copies of our book *Moratorium* to distribute to NDP folks. You don't have many visionary Social Gospel politicians like Tommy Douglas around these days…

I think CJL made a lasting impact with the combination of the Marshall Crowe decision and the moratorium proposal, which Mr. Berger recommended and Prime Minister Pierre Trudeau declared. It was quite a reversal for a government that initially decided to build the Mackenzie Valley pipeline. Those plans got set on their head. The moratorium is still in effect some 40 years later, as no pipeline has ever been built.

The pipeline struggle was a liberation struggle: a call to liberate energy decision making from a framework that considered the rights of the Dene and environmental rights as afterthoughts in a process dominated by the addiction to unfettered and uncaring economic growth.

Today, justice-minded and justice-driven Christians must continue to speak up and, as often as possible, do so in league with likeminded people and groups, or public policy will continue to be shaped by other worldviews – worldviews that more often put power before people and greed before caring for the marginalized and planet Earth. It continues to surprise me how many otherwise thoughtful people continue to believe in the trickle-down economy theory in the face of so much damaging evidence of the suffering that exposes that theory to be a gospel-denying myth.

I want to further reflect for a moment on CJL's decision to call for a moratorium on the Mackenzie Valley pipeline rather than outright opposition to its construction. A moratorium is a pause to allow for some serious consideration of the impacts and benefits of a project, to delve seriously into the proponents' stated rationale for the project, to consider scoping back, to consider alternatives and to discuss what really constitutes "Public Convenience and Necessity." It should also be a time for the Christian community to do its own reflection on what its shared gospel values might have to say about a proposed project. That happened to a limited extent in the case of the Mackenzie Valley proposal. Many people who worked for the oil and gas industry belonged to churches that sponsored Project North or were CJL members. There was negative feedback. I suppose there was less money in church collection plates. But in retrospect, the call for a moratorium was helpful in that it provided a less confrontational forum for discussion. It enabled a more collaborative consideration of the rights of the Dene Nation and their environment as well as the merits of a consumer-oriented society and what might constitute a more Just Energy Policy, including a more normative decision-making framework.

The focus of many church basement discussions was that the gospel leads to a different way of making public decisions than capitalism does. And that really mattered for our neighbours the Dene, and for their environment. It provided an opportunity to discuss the extent to which capitalism's values are institutionalized, not just in Parliament and the Legislative Assemblies, but consequently also in the decision-making boards and agencies established by those governments.

The CJL proposal for a Just Energy Policy included royalty and tax provisions to ensure that private companies develop public resources for public, rather than private, benefit, and that a portion of Canada's resources should be exported below international prices to struggling Third World countries. These continue to be very important priorities.

CJL tried hard to be courageous, and often threw caution to the winds. Today the churches as well as justice-oriented organizations like CPJ face new challenges: challenges to be more courageous than cautious in matters such as responding to the ever-louder call of justice for Indigenous peoples. Indigenous voices are telling us that first we took their land, and then we took their children. Although we say we are sorry we took their children, when will we return their lands that we illegally took from them, often through fraudulent pre-written Treaties?

Call to Action #46 of the Truth and Reconciliation Commission (TRC) calls all parties, including church parties to the Indian Residential School Settlement Agreement, to develop and sign a Covenant of Reconciliation that identifies principles for working collaboratively to advance reconciliation in Canadian society. That would include, but not be limited to, a list of matters including the following:

> (iv) support for the renewal or establishment of Treaty relationships based on principles of mutual recognition, mutual respect and shared responsibility for maintaining those relationships into the future.

The Very Reverend Stan McKay, Cree elder and former United Church Moderator, often reminds us that as Aboriginal and non-Aboriginal people, "we are all related." We are all Treaty partners. TRC call to action 46 (iv) is a call for non-Indigenous Treaty relatives to positively respond to our Aboriginal Treaty relatives who, in their Treaty areas, call for the establishment of Treaty renewal tables with Canada. The spirit and intent of the Treaties was to share land and resources with the newcomers – not to surrender them to the Crown.

The return of all traditional land is not realistic, and indeed many First Nation Treaty people are not calling for this. But some of it can be returned, and there can be resource revenue sharing and Indigenous consent for projects that are negotiated as part of renewed Treaties. The churches and all justice-minded people and organizations are called to be on the cutting edge, working hard to develop and sign Covenants of Reconciliation and advocating for Treaty renewal.

In 1976, Development and Peace (Catholic) and the Anglican Primate's World Relief and Development Fund loaned the Dene Nation $100,000 to pay for a crucial Assembly. The Dene later repaid the churches. It is with this spirit of open and welcoming arms that we should be reaching out to our First Nations relations today.

The Mackenzie Valley pipeline battle is an example of what can be done when folks set out in good faith to make gospel-based change. It doesn't all have to be planned at the beginning. There is a lot to be said for organic unfolding when like-minded folks put their hearts into a quest for justice.

In 1972, John Andrew Olthuis helped merge two groups into the CJL Foundation, which later became Citizens for Public Justice. He served there until 1989 and remains a proud member.

He is a founding partner at Olthuis/Kleer/Townshend, a firm of 30 lawyers based in Toronto and Yellowknife. He helped the Innu Nation of Labrador stop NATO low-level military flight training and the Grassy Narrows First Nation in their struggle against mercury pollution. He assisted the Assembly of First Nations' legal team in negotiating S.35 of Canada's Constitution Act 1982, and the 1992 Charlottetown Accord. John is an engaged member of Trinity St. Paul's United Church in Toronto.

CANADA'S CATHOLIC BISHOPS SPEAK OUT ABOUT ECONOMIC JUSTICE

Photo courtesy of Tony Clarke

INTERVIEW WITH TONY CLARKE

In the 1970s and 1980s, Canada's Catholic bishops regularly released pastoral letters on social themes. Most of these received "minor media coverage on the date of their release and little more after that," reported Joe Gunn and Monica Lambton in their 1999 book, Calling Out the Prophetic Tradition: A Jubilee of Social Teaching from the Canadian Conference of Catholic Bishops.

However, this was far from true when "Ethical Reflections on the Economic Crisis" was released on January 1, 1983.

"No other Church document in Canadian history ever created an equivalent reaction," said Social Affairs Commission member Bishop Remi De Roo. The statement was on the front

pages of daily newspapers across Canada. Within the first week, 19 editorials debated the declaration (11 in favour, six opposed), 16 public affairs programs on radio analyzed and dissected it, and 23 columnists wrote commentaries. The statement was covered in The New York Times, Washington Post, Los Angeles Times, Time *and* Newsweek. *In those pre-internet days, over 200,000 copies were circulated, and the text was eventually translated into seven languages.*

"Ethical Reflections" stung business leaders with its contention that the suffering of over 1.5 million unemployed in a struggling economy reflected a "moral disorder" in Canadian society. Public disaccord with the statement from the Archbishop of Toronto, Cardinal Emmett Carter, as well as Prime Minister Pierre Trudeau, only added to the debate.

Tony Clarke, then co-Director of the bishops' Social Affairs Office, helped to draft, and then defend, this statement, which remains a testament to how faith communities can frame necessary debates in Canadian society. Below, he remembers some of the dynamics at play at that time.

There had been a history of Labour Day statements from Canada's Roman Catholic bishops, and they were often quite successful, such as 1975's "Northern Development: At What Cost?" and in 1976, "From Words to Action." Statements like these had rejuvenated the social teachings in the Canadian Catholic Church. During this period, for example, a number of dioceses set up social action offices, and a network of social justice initiatives began to develop across the country. The Canadian Conference of Catholic Bishops (CCCB) also started to subdivide its work into the Western region, Ontario, Quebec, and the Atlantic region.

In each of those four regions, we had a sufficient nucleus of social justice offices and activities that could be organized on a more local and regional level. Also, at the CCCB, we had a very strong Social Affairs Commission at that time. It was made up of eight bishops from the four regions of the country who were keen on pursuing this ministry.

In the early 1980s, there was a downturn in the economy. Inflation had risen very sharply, but so had unemployment. And most of this was being borne by people who were on the margins of society and of the economy. At Commission meetings we would get reports, responses and reactions to what was going on back in the bishops' own communities and dioceses. They described a deepening concern, especially among those who were unemployed, people experiencing poverty and some real human suffering. We also did a little outreach to bishops who were not on the Commission to see whether something similar had been experienced elsewhere, and we found that indeed, it was the case. So we came to the conclusion that something needed to be done.

Originally, we weren't thinking of another statement. Instead, we proposed sending a letter to the prime minister. But then, as the crisis deepened, it made more sense to make use of John Paul II's latest encyclical, "On Human Work" (*Laborem Exercens*, September 1981), which had broken new ground in Catholic Social Teaching. With this encyclical, the letter could be reframed as an episcopal statement.

In the fall of 1982, we began to turn the draft from a letter to the prime minister into a public statement. The question was when should we release it. Finally, in a conversation with the general secretary, me, the president of the bishops' conference and the chair of the Social Affairs Commission (Bishop Remi De Roo), we finally made a decision that it would be released officially on January 1 as a New Year's statement.

In terms of the content, "Ethical Reflections" was a statement based upon two basic ethical priorities. The first was "the preferential option for the poor," which was an ethical principle that had arisen out of liberation theology and was something we had adopted in our work in the Social Affairs Commission.

Here it was applied to the widening gap between the rich and poor and the concentration of wealth in the hands of a few.

The second principle was "the priority of human labour." Recognizing that work gives a person dignity means people take precedence over the dictates of capital and of technology. So, taken together, these principles were summarized as follows: "the needs of the poor have priority over the wants of the rich, the rights of workers are more important than profit, and the participation of the marginalized takes precedence over an economic order that excludes them."

The second theme of the document acknowledged the human suffering we had witnessed – massive layoffs due to the downturn in the economy, abandoned one-industry towns, cutbacks in health and social services, growing line-ups at local soup kitchens, and the kind of emotional stress that went along with all of this, resulting in family breakups and suicides. We identified different sectors that were particularly hard hit: unemployed people on social assistance, the working poor, and of course women, Indigenous people, pensioners, young people, small producers, and so on…

A third theme focused on the nature of the economic crisis itself. There had been a structural shift in Canada's economy. Prime Minister Pierre Trudeau had gone on national television three times in what *The Globe and Mail* called "a series of sermonettes." He talked about the global economy and how Canada had to restructure for a new global era. While the prime minister was right in saying there was an economic crisis, his solutions, in our view, were heading down the wrong path. At least, this was our operating assumption.

The transnational corporations and banks combined the computerization of technology to create what Trudeau called "a tough new world of global competition." As he put it in his sermonettes, we've got to rejig ourselves and our economy under this enormous global competition, and it's going to be tough. But the bishops replied, saying [more or less], "Hold it, wait a minute, there are a lot of implications to what you're proposing here. You're not talking about the problems that are being faced by workers, by the unemployed, those living with widespread poverty, etc."

The fourth theme focused on the emerging "moral disorder." By making inflation the number one problem over that of unemployment, the government was putting greater emphasis on the accumulation of profit and machines than on people who actually work in the economy. And so the value and dignity of human work were violated. In doing so, the bishops declared, government had incorporated principles of Social Darwinism, namely, the survival of the fittest, thereby creating a society of winners and losers.

Instead, as a fifth theme, government strategies focused on taming inflation. By seeing the private sector as the engine of recovery, they adopted wage and price controls. To us, this suggested another dimension of the moral disorder. After all, Trudeau had defeated the Conservatives in the 1980 election by saying he would never bring in wage and price controls – and then he did! In short, this strategy for economic recovery targeted the vulnerable more than the more powerful.

The sixth theme had to do with alternative approaches. Here, the bishops tried to point out that the government, led by the big business community, offered one "solution," but there were alternatives. We proposed that the priorities be turned around by starting with the people who are really suffering as a result of these policies, and make sure that their needs trump the maximization of profit and excessive growth as the supreme goals of the economy. The government and its allies kept saying that the levels of unemployment in the country were normal and natural. The bishops disagreed; these policies were human made and caused by the economic policies and strategies that were imposed. Massive unemployment deprives people of their human dignity and an adequate income. In effect, this was a form of social evil that needed to be tackled.

Theme seven discussed economic recovery. Unemployment, rather than just inflation, should be treated as a major obstacle to economic recovery. What was missing was an industrial strategy to create permanent and meaningful jobs on a regional and community basis. Canada needed an equitable and balanced program to fight inflation, which implied maintaining and improving our social programs. And, finally, labour unions needed to be invited to play a more decisive role in developing strategies for economic recovery and employment.

Then, the statement went on to declare that our economic model was capital intensive, using less and less human labour; second, it was largely energy intensive, requiring more and more non-renewable energy resources; and third, it was export oriented, designed to serve market demands elsewhere rather than basic needs at home. These points drew considerable wrath from government and big business officials.

Theme nine was about participatory democracy. Basically, people had been forgotten and were not listened to. Maybe the working people in our communities didn't have a detailed understanding of what needed to happen, but they certainly had some impulses that needed to be heard.

Finally, moral responsibility. We can't just critique. We must act – as Christians, as churches and as faith communities. There was interest in organizing public forums and workshops to discuss and debate the major issues of economic justice facing each region of the country. Churches and faith-based communities need to play a role in helping to make this happen. In this context, the moral crisis and the relationship between ethics and economics could be explored and debated further.

So, these were the main pillars of "Ethical Reflections on the Economic Crisis" in 1983.

You know, the best-kept secret of the Catholic Church is its own social teachings. Three things happened in 1982–83. First, there was a convergence of the fundamental principles of our Catholic heritage. These have a powerful message for how to organize society and the economy. The social teachings came through a number of papal teachings, but they were refined and reworked by the Commission's methodology.

Second, economic realities had reached a real crisis in Canada. A year or so before the statement, there was a huge gathering on Parliament Hill of 100,000 people protesting the wage and price control policy. The government turned its back on them and walked away. The big business community formed the Business Council on National Issues (BCNI) in the 1970s, comprised of the leading 150 CEOs of large companies. They were well organized, and they had the ear of government. It was the early stages of what some of us would call the rise of the corporate agenda, the rise of corporate rule in the country.

And then there was the real suffering of the people… The moral message of the bishops was powerful, due to their pastoral methodology. That pastoral message started by listening.

"Ethical Reflections" surprised people and caught them off guard. But it struck a chord with people who were feeling marginalized. One of the best examples I remember came from Jim Sinclair, the leader of the Fisherman's Union on the west coast. He called me shortly after the statement came out and said, "Our people just came off the boat and said, 'The bishops are on our side, the bishops are on our side!'" They felt validated by the fact that someone had listened to their plight (even though it wasn't specifically about fishers). "Ethical Reflections" touched people who were outcasts due to the policies of that time.

Toronto's Archbishop, Emmett Carter, inadvertently helped "Ethical Reflections" have legs. He heard it reported on CBC national TV on December 31. The Archbishop, who was working at his desk, immediately reacted, even though he would have known of it, as he was on the CCCB's Administrative Board. (The Commission approved drafts and passed them on according to procedure at the CCCB. We couldn't write a letter, much less send it, without the Executive of the Conference approving it in principle, and that is exactly what happened. But the Archbishop was not pleased.)

He called a press conference the next day. On January 1, I got a call from Tom Harpur of the *Toronto Star*, saying, "I've got good news and bad news. The good news is have you seen the front cover of the *Toronto Star* yet?" I said no. He said, "Well, you should." (His infamous story, which I have right in front of me now, was called "Canada's Unemployed Immoral, Bishops Charge." It had a big picture of an unemployed worker on the front page.)

He said this story was having ripple effects everywhere, and then the second thing he said was "Archbishop Carter has called a press conference, and the word is that he's going to blast it." So, I got in touch with the CCCB general secretary and kept him informed. But everybody was cool with it, because protocol had been followed.

Meanwhile, Trudeau was in Bangkok at that time, on a trade mission to Southeast Asia. He held a press conference about his trip, and the first question was about the bishops' statement. Trudeau famously said, "Well, the cat has been thrown among the pigeons; I'll leave it to the bishops to fight it out."

Carter didn't win any major support in the bishops' conference on this. Support for the CCCB Executive and for the president was maintained, and the Commission was begrudgingly vindicated. Later, Bill Ryan (head of the Jesuits) went to his old friend Carter and convinced him that he should have his own hearings in his own diocese to see if "Ethical Reflections" was backed up by what was happening in Toronto. George

Ignatieff (Chancellor of the University of Toronto) chaired those hearings at the Renaissance Hotel in Scarborough. His final report, *Canada's Unemployed: The Crisis of Our Times*, read like a vindication of the bishops' New Year's statement. Media coverage of "Ethical Reflections" went on for 11 days straight. That's pretty significant. David MacDonald, who had been in the Conservative Cabinet of Joe Clark, told me at the time that if a story went for two or three days and had some life in the first, second or third page of mainline newspapers, it was good. If it went six days, it was really good, and if it went more than six or nine days, then it was a story that would carry for the rest of the year. At the end of 1983, we were still getting coverage of this year-old pastoral letter!

The ecumenical response to the pastoral letter was remarkably positive, on the surface. Specific supporting statements were made by Anglican Primate Ted Scott, by United Church Moderator Clark Macdonald and by Eileen Smith on the part of the Presbyterians. Lutheran David Pfrimmer organized a big event in Waterloo, where I went to speak. Even so, the public uproar and attention was a matter of ecumenical sensitivity. Other churches had spoken out and taken a stand on various issues of economic justice in the past. So, when the bishops' New Year's Eve declaration was released amid public fanfare, it ran the risk of stealing their thunder. Thankfully, the possibility of a major cleavage with the other churches was averted, largely because of the serious ecumenical work that had been done through a decade of interchurch collaboration on social justice matters.

The process around preparing "Ethical Reflections," and then the huge response to it, gave rise to many lessons. We learned that, to impact government, we needed to build alliances with different sectors of society to create strong coalitional forces. In those days, the churches writ large were taken somewhat seriously as potential players in the process of bringing about economic and social change.

In 1986, for example, something called "Dialogue 86" was organized to promote "social dialogue" between big business, government and labour unions. During this Dialogue '86, Bishop Adolphe Proulx from the CCCB Social Affairs Commission made an intervention in which he basically questioned how labour unions could achieve their goals by getting into bed with big business, which has different values and priorities. That message sent reverberations everywhere. Eventually, we were able to wean the labour movement away from its dependence on this dialogue with big business in the BCNI. As a result, the Action Canada Network, which was organized in 1987 as an umbrella alliance of civil society groups opposed to free trade with the US [and later NAFTA], did not include a partnership of any kind with either big business or the government.

Unfortunately, "Ethical Reflections" didn't have as much impact inside the church itself. That may have been more our fault, in that we didn't follow up with a strong internal strategy. Perhaps that would not have gone very far anyway, since many Catholics still don't see the social teachings as part of their identity as Catholics.

Nevertheless, I wouldn't want to underestimate the impact inside. For a while, "Ethical Reflections" gave a lot of weight to those who were carrying the social justice banner in the church. They felt vindicated, either directly or indirectly, as a result of what happened. Some even commented that it opened up new doors for them that they hadn't had before.

But several others preferred to work only inside the Catholic community, with Development & Peace and with the social action offices. Some didn't want to develop relationships with people from various civil society organizations, like unions or the anti-poverty movement – instead, most of their alliances were within the institution. Despite the fact that they had something enormous to contribute to both, they did not develop those relationships and friendships with social movement people outside the institution.

To be sure, there was some ongoing support for "Ethical Reflections" in the CCCB, but structural reorganizations were soon implemented. From Rome, Pope John Paul II wanted bishops' conferences around the world to have less autonomy. The backbone was largely removed from our work. Eventually, Cardinal Carter became president of the CCCB, where he constantly reminded everyone that this should never happen again. I wrote about this in 1995 in *Behind the Mitre: The Moral Leadership Crisis in the Canadian Catholic Church.*

For example, when the McDonald Commission (on the future of the Canadian economy) wanted to have a special hearing with the bishops' conference, the only people allowed into the meeting were the president of the CCCB, and the two general secretaries (English and French). For all intents and purposes, the bishops and staff of the Social Affairs Commission, who authored "Ethical Reflections," were excluded.

I think a similar statement should and could be made today. Anytime you bring ethics and economics together, you have an opportunity to open up a world of understanding for people. That's really important.

Although the economy has changed a great deal since those days – becoming, for example, much more globalized, it never ceases to amaze me how much it remains the same. Today, the ecological challenge is much more powerful and real than it was then. Therefore, the alliances that we'd reach out to, the organized and unorganized workers, but also Indigenous people and leading environmental movements, would have a more prominent role to play. But reflecting back on those 10 parts of "Ethical Reflections," I'm amazed at how much of that is still relevant.

Looking at the economy and society from an ethical perspective and being motivated by the relationship with human suffering is a powerful thing. "From Words to Action" was really a pastoral methodology for doing social justice. It starts by listening to the cries of the marginalized and the oppressed. You listen to those who are suffering. We could not have written "Ethical Reflections" had we not done "From Words to Action." In another statement, "A Society to Be Transformed," there were things that made a breakthrough. Today, "Northern Development: At What Cost?" would add a lot more momentum to the ecological shift.

Before people of faith speak out on matters of injustice, they need to adhere to a methodology similar to that which Jesus followed. He listened first to the people most directly affected. Then you can analyze the situation and identify the causes before making moral judgments and proceeding with follow-up actions to overcome the injustice. The point here is that this voice must not be lost. It's a voice that can help reawaken the poor, marginalized and oppressed peoples of our times to the point where they can put forward their own demands for what needs to be done to transform society, thereby overcoming today's ongoing social, economic and ecological injustices.

Tony Clarke worked for the CCCB from 1972 until 1994. He helped create and chair Project North, chaired the Justice and Peace Commission of the Canadian Council of Churches, and was elected national chair of the Action Canada Network, which led the struggle against free trade. In 1994, Tony co-organized a successful international campaign to stop the Multilateral Agreement on Investment. In 1997, he founded the Polaris Institute to challenge the power of corporations. He holds a B.A. from the University of British Columbia and master's and doctoral degrees from the University of Chicago. He is the author [or co-author] of 11 books. In 2005, Tony received the Right Livelihood Award, known as Sweden's Alternative Nobel Prize.

CANADIAN CHURCHES OPPOSE APARTHEID IN SOUTH AFRICA

Photo by Lauren King

INTERVIEW WITH MOIRA HUTCHINSON

Anglican Archbishop Desmond Tutu, winner of the 1985 Nobel Peace Prize, has stated that apartheid could not have been defeated in his native South Africa without the imposition of international financial sanctions. Canada, at the time, had a trade and investment profile in the country approaching $377 million. Some of the country's largest companies had investments there, and Canadian banks provided important loans.

In December 1972, the Catholic bishops and the Canadian Council of Churches (then comprised of only Protestant denominations) established an ad hoc taskforce to research the activity of corporations in the Global South and the moral dimensions of conducting business there. This resulted in the forming of an ecumenical coalition called the Taskforce on the Churches and Corporate Responsibility (TCCR) in January 1975.

TCCR's first coordinator was Renate Pratt, who in 1973 had authored the first study of Canadian economic links with South Africa, called Investment in Oppression. *TCCR researched and acted on Canadian corporate involvement: for example, providing stickers that read "No Loans to South Africa" and "No Loans to Chile" which could be affixed to cheques. Member churches and religious congregations participating in the Taskforce were the first Canadian investors to raise social justice questions at annual meetings of shareholders.*

In 1978, the Royal Bank pledged to halt loans, and "in early 1980 the Toronto Dominion became the first Canadian bank to announce an unconditional halt to new loans and to any renewal of loans to South Africa's government and its agencies." TCCR takes credit for this happening long before the Conservative government in Ottawa included a "voluntary" ban on private loans to South Africa in 1985. The next year, Ottawa issued more, largely symbolic, economic and diplomatic sanctions. The Taskforce's work to challenge corporate Canada's support of apartheid is detailed in a wonderful 1997 volume written by Renate Pratt, In Good Faith: Canadian Churches Against Apartheid, *and is told in Moira Hutchinson's words.*

I came on staff at the Taskforce on the Churches and Corporate Responsibility (TCCR) on a half-time basis in 1981. Renate Pratt had been its coordinator since 1975, with just an assistant secretary. I was really excited by this position. The churches wanted to expand their work into energy and environmental issues, so I focused on these. However, I also worked closely with Renate on the South Africa file, which was such a huge part of the agenda, and on human rights in Latin America. The environmental agenda was focused on forestry and mining issues in Canada, especially where the rights of First Nations were involved. It was a broad agenda.

TCCR was started by six churches, six religious orders (which eventually swelled to 18) and two religious federations. Tom Anthony of the Anglican Church was the founding chair. Later chairs included Jack Zimmerman (Lutheran), Jim Webb (Jesuit), Brian Fraser (Presbyterian Church), Tim Ryan (Scarboro Foreign Missions), Bill Davis (United Church), Ann Abraham (Anglican Church), Sheila Kappler (Ursulines of the Chatham Union) and Ray Hodgson (Presbyterian Church). In the early years, there were also consultative members, like LAWG (the Latin American Working Group), TCLSAC (Toronto Committee for the Liberation of Southern African Colonies), CUSO and the YWCA.

In deciding to form a shareholder coalition, the churches were influenced by the example of the Interfaith Center on Corporate Responsibility in the US. The Center had been doing shareholder action on corporate responsibility in relation to the war in Vietnam and apartheid in South Africa.

The Board members had to be very hands on. I mean, we had this huge agenda and less than two full-time program staff, so it meant that the Board members themselves, who were mostly staff from the churches and religious communities, did a lot of work.

TCCR was a bit different from some of the other ecumenical coalitions. When we were dealing with major corporations and representing church shareholders, we were very clear that our actions were not being taken as TCCR. Maybe only a couple of the members held shares in a specific company, and only those members spoke on behalf of their institutions at annual meetings. But we did seek the consensus of all the members on actions taken. We had to be very careful to remind Board reps of their responsibility to check back with their denomination, because we couldn't be caught out pretending to represent the pension fund or the investment fund of one of the churches if the proposal hadn't gone through due processes within that church.

When I came to TCCR, we were just on the edge of a breakthrough in the tools we had at our disposal. The Canada Business Corporations Act was changed, so that made it possible for minority shareholders to file a proposal. Before that, a shareholder had to hold 5 percent of the company's shares to have the right to submit a proposal – a threshold so high that even major pension funds seldom hold that much in a single company. A proposal is circulated to all the shareholders prior to the annual meeting, and shareholders vote on it through the proxy document in advance of the meeting, or at the meeting.

The right to have a proposal circulated gets your issue right into the centre of the company's universe. Before that, if a company refused to meet with us, or refused to consider any changes, our only recourse was to ask questions from the floor of the annual meeting, which is attended by only a small percentage of shareholders. I must say, though, that in those days the churches had enough clout in the community that companies did not ignore requests for meetings easily. We usually got meetings with the CEO and others in those days. Not so much later…

It was this change in the Canada Business Corporations Act that allowed the churches to file the first minority shareholder proposal ever put forward in Canada, and that led directly – after several efforts – to Alcan's decision in 1986 to disinvest from South Africa.

Our preparation for meetings with companies was an important part of our work. We never spoke to the media or at an annual meeting without first having made attempts (usually successful) to meet with the company itself. That was incredibly important. We often found that we gleaned information that they didn't realize they were giving us, or we corrected information that was slightly wrong and could have been embarrassing if we had used it.

After the Soweto massacre on June 16, 1976, when 200,000 black students took to the streets of that neighbourhood to protest the imposition of *Afrikaans* as the medium of instruction, and at least 176 protestors were killed, the work on South Africa became even more intense. Some of the important opposition to TCCR's work came from Canadian companies and banks, but also, more subtly, from the Department of External Affairs. Also, an organization was formed to counter TCCR's work – the Confederation of Church and Business People (CCBP), established in Toronto by several Noranda Corporation businessmen, a retired United Church Moderator, some retired Anglican bishops and various clergy. They hired Rev. Charles Plaskett to counter TCCR's questioning of corporations, and Project North's call for a moratorium on frontier oil and gas projects. Ron Willoughby, CCBP chair, was Imperial Oil's manager of public affairs. It didn't figure hugely in our work, because quite wisely, our Board decided that they would respond themselves to their church members who were circulating CCBP information. We were aware of CCBP activities, but its opposition wasn't as important as what the companies themselves were doing.

We were right there in their faces. Canadian companies were incredibly fearful about having critics speak from within the corporate circle. Church investors dared to come to annual meetings to ask questions, or even worse, church investors filed shareholder proposals. That was very new in Canada. Company spokespersons and shareholders who were friendly to church investors often said, "Why don't you just sell your shares if you don't like what we're doing?"

That's what they really wanted, because then we would be gone. To try to prevent the churches from invading this corporate space, companies used a couple of tactics. Early on, the reception of church shareholders at annual meetings was sometimes quite hostile. For example, on one occasion, when a church representative was in the midst of asking a question from the floor of an annual meeting of a bank, the chairman actually shut off the mike!

But that was a minor tactic. A more serious form of opposition was legal. I was the TCCR coordinator when Varity Corporation (formerly Massey Ferguson, where Conrad Black had been the CEO) went to court in a very unusual pre-emptive attempt to prevent church shareholders from filing a proposal. The proposal asked Varity to terminate its investments in South Africa. We lost the court case, and then appealed because of the important precedent it set regarding shareholder rights in Canada. We lost the appeal as well – two to one. The outcome, however, is a complicated story. Because Varity also sold shares in the United States, where laws were friendlier to shareholders, Varity had to abide by US rules. The Securities and Exchange Commission (SEC) there forced it to circulate our proposal.

There was another legal effort, this time by Shell Canada, to prevent the circulation of a church proposal. And again, the Securities and Exchange Commission (SEC) insisted that they circulate the proposal. But Shell went ahead and sent out its proxy materials anyway, without including our proposal. We agreed not to force the issue if Shell made lots of time available to us to explain our concerns at their annual meeting in Calgary. Instead, they treated us with contempt. But Shell may have regretted their actions because after the meeting, the media flocked to me to ask what was going on and I told the whole story that night on the CBC Radio program "As It Happens."

Another corporate effort to undermine a shareholder proposal involved the Canadian Imperial Bank of Commerce (CIBC). It wouldn't tell us what kind of loans it made to South Africa. We filed a shareholder proposal seeking disclosure of its foreign loans over a specified threshold that would include its loans to South Africa. That proposal actually had a lot of institutional shareholder support, because we were just seeking a level of disclosure that was already required in the US. As the votes came in, the bank saw that some of its shareholders were voting against management and for the churches. On the pretext that these shareholders might have been confused by the layout of the voting document, the bank started phoning them to "verify" their intentions. We found out about this when *The Globe and Mail* wrote a story about it after a call from a shareholder sympathetic to TCCR. We followed up the next year with a proposal to the CIBC asking it to develop a secret ballot protocol, and we made secret ballot proposals to several other companies as well. The companies almost all agreed. How could you not agree that your ballot should be secret? I know that sounds like not very sexy stuff in terms of social responsibility, but it is. Improvements in corporate governance help to level the playing field between management and shareholders and other stakeholders – another legacy of our anti-apartheid shareholder campaign.

Another important part of TCCR's work was advocacy with governments. TCCR was doing both government and corporate advocacy on South Africa together, and for very good reasons. We wanted to have the framework for corporate activity set by the government, but sometimes found that if one or two companies stuck their necks out and responded to our requests, this would raise the bar, and we could ratchet up the expectations for government regulation or policy. So there was an important relationship between the two elements of the advocacy campaigns of TCCR.

The work with government was no easier than with companies. External Affairs, while sometimes seeming to be responsive to our efforts, systematically minimized action on our recommendations. Our briefs were exceptionally well researched and we didn't back off, but we had to be incredibly persistent, going back and back.

Overall, the federal government's record on South Africa was mixed. Renate Pratt gave credit to Prime Minister Brian Mulroney for actions that were taken to help move the Commonwealth to administer sanctions, and several TCCR recommendations were adopted at that time. But certainly, Canada's later pullback was disappointing. When the government did act, it was something "like pushing on an open door," as Renate put it. In other words, the banks had already stopped making loans to South Africa before the government announced the policy that the banks shouldn't make loans there.

I have a favourite story about government efforts to avoid action. I was involved in the research into South Africa's illegal occupation of Namibia, and the Canadian government's refusal to acknowledge the illegality of the occupation through its own policies. There was uranium coming from Namibia to Canada for processing at Eldorado Nuclear (a Crown corporation at the time). This should not have been happening – the resources of Namibia were being depleted under an illegal regime: South Africa. Jim Webb, the Jesuit representative to TCCR, had contact with some trade unionists who worked on the docks where the uranium was being imported. Through them, we learned the uranium was coming into Canada with the country of origin listed as South Africa. The Canadian government was, in effect, granting that South Africa owned Namibia, or controlled Namibia legally. So, we pointed this out to the government. Its response? It changed the designation on the import documents to read "country of export" instead of "country of origin." These little bureaucratic tricks were used to try to get around the objections we were raising to their policies.

Another TCCR campaign was focused on the International Monetary Fund, which was giving credits and making loans available to South Africa. To my astonishment, when I went home to visit my 82-year-old mother, who was an active member of an Anglican women's group, I heard that all the women in her group had written letters to the Minister of Finance, because Canada had voted in favour of these loans. You think an issue is too complicated for people, and then you find out that your 82-year-old mother has written a letter about it. I was just so pleased – and she hadn't even found out about the issue from me!

Corporate and government advocacy was only a part of the effort to end apartheid. The churches were engaged, individually and jointly, in education and solidarity activities. In 1982, the Inter-Church Coalition on Africa was established, and it shared office space with us. It took up work on South Africa in 1985, and played an important role in grassroots mobilization. TCCR also worked closely with other church and secular partners. For example, Project Ploughshares provided assistance related to arms exports to South Africa. Ken Luckhardt and Ken Taynor, the staff of the South African Congress of Trade Unions Solidarity Committee, were the experts on trade.

It was important for Canadian anti-apartheid work when, at the end of 1985, Anglican Primate Ted Scott was named to the seven-person Eminent Persons Group of the Commonwealth. Returning from South Africa, where he twice met Nelson Mandela, the Primate became a key advisor to Prime Minister Mulroney and External Affairs Minister Joe Clark. Scott believed that "Sanctions and peace for South Africa had become one and the same thing."

I remember meeting Archbishop Tutu with a small group of Canadian church activists. That was pretty special on a personal level. And it was a great tribute to Renate that he wrote the preface to her book *In Good Faith: Canadian Churches Against Apartheid*. I also remember attending a banquet for hundreds of people when Nelson Mandela came to Toronto in June 1990, after his release from prison, to thank Canadians for our support and solidarity. This might sound negative, but I thought, "Where were all these people when the work was so tough?"

People sometimes ask about the theological basis for TCCR's work. In the case of South Africa, we were certainly united in opposition to the position of the Dutch Reformed Church in South Africa, which argued on their reading of Genesis 11 that God wanted people divided into separate races. However, in general within TCCR there was not a lot of theological discussion. Each church approached the issues we addressed within its own theological framework. We recognized the importance of the 1985 Kairos Document of Black theologians, but our focus was on the ways in which we could work together. The different histories, relationships and theological perspectives of the churches meant that there were initially some differences among them on policies regarding comprehensive sanctions, with some having stronger positions than others. However, there was strong support from the beginning for ending loans and ending strategic investments that undercut the arms embargo.

TCCR learned important lessons from this work. The resistance led by the African National Congress in South Africa was the primary force for change, with economic sanctions contributing to the process leading to negotiations. The imposition of sanctions was encouraged through the investor campaigns – and among those campaigns, I believe that in Canada, shareholder action by investors, not divestment, had the greatest impact.

There is an important distinction to be made between trying to get companies to disinvest from South Africa, and divestment by investors. An investor may divest shares, but it hasn't necessarily accomplished the end goal of getting the company to disinvest. Both divestment and shareholder action could have an impact. However, some of those who divested and walked away with "clean hands" were then silent. Also, even a large institution's divestment had little or no direct financial impact on a company.

While there continues to be debate about the relative importance of divestment and shareholder engagement, in the case of South Africa, it was the month-after-month, year-after-year persistence of the church shareholders, raising questions with the companies, that had the most impact. The process of repeated engagement with the companies not only had an impact on the actions of those companies, but perhaps more importantly, it informed our understanding of the apartheid system and its supports. This understanding then focused and sharpened the recommendations we made to government for sanctions.

One of the long-term impacts of the South Africa campaign has been to broaden the constituency of investors who are interested in what it means to be an "ethical" or "responsible" investor. They want to be active investors, rather than just passively screening their investments. It's a great development that there is now a strong coalition, SHARE (Shareholder Association for Research and Education), composed not only of faith-based organizations, but also pension funds, ethical mutual funds, and foundations. Its founding and current executive director is Peter Chapman. Peter worked with me at TCCR.

The churches and religious communities have fewer resources, and in the context of Canadian society have far less clout with governments or corporations than they did 20 or 30 years ago. However, now, through SHARE, they have more allies. These shareholders have generally screened out certain kinds of investments initially, such as in tobacco, arms and pornography, but they also engage with the companies in their portfolios on a broad range of other issues.

SHARE also continues the TCCR example of advocacy with government on policies and regulations shaping corporate behaviour. That advocacy continues to be informed by the persistent work of engaging with corporations.

Shareholder engagement is hard work. It takes time and energy and attention to be an engaged shareholder. It's much easier to sell your shares. And sometimes you can be engaged for a long time and see very little progress – and in that case, you might decide to divest. But in other cases, when you keep at it, there is positive change, and it's worth the effort.

Moira Hutchinson was staff and then coordinator of TCCR, organizing national events on ethical investment funds, community investment and active shareholdership. After, Moira promoted socially responsible investment as a consultant with NGOs and unions. Her briefs to Industry Canada opened the way to important federal corporate law reforms in 2001.

Moira has served as chair of the Canadian Alternative Investment Committee, the Maquila Solidarity Network, and Project Ploughshares; on the Board of Transfair Canada; and on the investment committees of the Atkinson Charitable Foundation and the United Church of Canada.

She received an award from the Social Investment Organization in 1991, the Queen's University Alumni Achievement Award in 2000, and the Canadian Responsible Investment Distinguished Service Award in 2013.

NORTHERN CANADIAN BISHOPS RESPOND TO VIOLENCE AGAINST WOMEN

Photo by Lorna Dall

INTERVIEW WITH MARIE ZAROWNY, SSA

Some Canadian churches, even those that speak out strongly on contemporary issues, still display an evident blind spot when it comes to the issue of gender equality. This contradiction has hurt the public credibility of the churches' message, rendering it less than authentic to many North American ears, especially among women and the young.

Ecumenical organizations have often had a different leadership history. The Canadian Council of Churches has had more than one woman serve as general secretary and president, and

KAIROS – Canadian Ecumenical Justice Initiatives has had several women serve as executive director.

Yet Canadian church and ecumenical statements often do not emphasize a specific gender analysis in their social teaching.

And whereas all Christian churches highlight the role of the family, not all have paid attention to the issue of conjugal violence. Some misused interpretations of Scripture have even contributed to situations where women have been advised to stay in violent relationships, in spite of danger to their own well-being and that of their children.

The United Nations defines violence against women as "Any act of gender-based violence that results in, or is likely to result in, physical, sexual or psychological harm or suffering to women, including threats of such acts, coercion or arbitrary deprivation of liberty, whether occurring in public or in private life."

One innovative project to address family violence was begun in northern Canada in the 1990s. This novel effort culminated in a series of three statements by Catholic bishops of the North, ongoing commitments to address domestic violence, and the raising of consciousness among church members. The story of this work is recounted here by Sr. Marie Zarowny, the project leader.

Upon the recommendation of Fr. René Fumoleau, Bishop Denis Croteau OMI invited me to work in the diocese of Yellowknife in 1987. My task was to complete a study of the political, economic and social changes that were occurring in the North, and to do some social analysis and theological reflection. That provided me with an amazing opportunity to visit every one of the 22 communities in the diocese at that time. Many of them were fly-in, so I'd end up staying for days at a time, interviewing people and attending all the meetings that were happening. That was an amazing experience of immersion in the cultures and issues of the North.

Out of this process emerged a study called "Walking Together." My intention was to stay in the diocese to implement the recommendations on how the church could be more supportive of the aspirations of the people. The bishop asked me to help organize a diocesan Synod, and so this document became a key pillar of that two-and-a-half year process. Following the Synod, I worked on implementing those recommendations. Then, wanting to reinsert myself in one of the communities, I lived in Fort Simpson for a year, supporting the lay leaders there and doing some writing.

But Bishop Croteau approached me again with his vision that the bishops across the North needed to speak out publicly together on issues of common concern. That was the dream. The bishops of the North asked me to facilitate a workshop with them, to decide if they wanted to do that, and if so, what exactly they would focus on.

The bishops concluded after our workshop that they wanted to do something together, and since 1994 was International Year of the Family, they'd focus on family life. I was a bit concerned that this project would be hijacked by the "family values" stream in the church, so I suggested to them, based on the social teaching of the church, that they might want to consider the broader context of society in which the family was inserted. So out of that emerged this project called "Family and Society North."

The focus was to see what was going on in society that impacted family, especially the destructive impacts, and discover if there were things that the bishops could do or publicly speak out against. The other side of it was how could families themselves have an impact on the wider society? And what kind of supports would families need to do that – since we all know that families are the keystone of society, no?

I was asked to coordinate this work for three years. I continued living in Yellowknife, but was hired by the eight dioceses of the North. Each of the bishops wanted me to visit his diocese and communities to meet with pastoral workers, priests and families. The methodology of the project was to have each diocese name a leader who was to coordinate and spearhead work there. I would work with that person and each bishop. During that first year, I visited a number of communities (some more than once), making sure I met with diocesan pastoral leaders, diocesan staff and social service agencies in each locale. I had a chance during those community visits to go door to door to meet with families – that's what you do in the North – and of course I had practice in doing that, as this was what I had done when undertaking my original study in the Yellowknife diocese. Meeting people one on one and talking, going to the various offices, the nursing station, the counselling department, going to the school and talking to the principal and some of the teachers, going to the chief and councillors. And in the non-Indigenous communities it was through the church that I met with people, organized through the parishes. I had a process of reflection that I engaged people in; that was basically the method.

When the diocese of Labrador celebrated its 50th anniversary, the bishops of the North had their meeting there. I was invited to do my interviews in the diocese about two weeks before, and then gave a report on the project to the assembled bishops at that meeting. The issue of violence in the home had come up in virtually every place I visited, no matter who I talked to. It was quite depressing! These things are deeply embedded in my memory… One of the women said, "If the bishops want to do anything about helping families in the North, they have to get the men to stop beating us up."

There were clear, strong statements. I remember another woman in the Labrador diocese said, "Our priest is really good; he's kind, he speaks all the time about how God loves us, he really encourages us … but you know, what we would like to hear from him, even once, is that Jesus would not want you men to be beating up your wives."

I thought, "Well, these are doable things..."

I was on fire by the time I met with the bishops. I was so upset by everything that I had heard... I no longer have a copy of the report I gave to them, but I remember just laying it on them, including the Apostolic Delegate (Rome's Nuncio appointed to Canada), who was just dumbfounded. I asked them, "What do priests learn in seminaries, if a man comes to them and says he beat up his wife? What do you say to them? Does anybody even think this is a sin, you know, to beat up your partner? Or anybody?" And one of the bishops said to me afterwards, that in all his years as a pastor, not once had a man come to him and admitted to beating up his wife. I responded that I could hardly believe it. The bishop explained, what they've said is that they "got angry with her." And he never thought of going further, asking, "Well, what did you do in your anger?"

Another bishop said to me, "You know, I thought I knew the people in my diocese... women come and talk to me all the time about things... none of them has ever talked this passionately about violence." So, I said to him, "That's why you need a woman to go out there; they aren't going to say it to you."

They had their eyes opened and were moved to do something. There were about five issues that arose in my conversations in the communities, but the strongest was this issue of family violence. The bishops collectively chose then to move forward to address that.

We also had two conferences over these years, as part of the project, with the bishop and the person who was spearheading the project in each diocese, and several families participating, too. They were excellent events. I remember that one was held in Winnipeg. Greg Dunwoody helped me facilitate that event.

It was the bishops' idea that we write these pastoral statements. I drafted something based on what I had heard and sent it to the bishops, and then most of them sent it to the person whom they had asked to coordinate this work in their diocese. Some sent it to all their pastoral leaders, and then they collected their feedback and sent it back to me. Based on this feedback, I revised the documents and sent them back again. So it was a cumbersome method, but I think it helped give them ownership of it.

The process was consultative and collaborative. Of course, I'm generally more interested in the process than I am in the conclusion, because I think the process is what leads to effective action at the end. You know, if you don't have ownership, and people involved in it, then folks could care less… The bishops were fabulous to work with; they could not have been better. What I appreciated about working with them is that they were all missionaries at heart, and really, all they were interested in was the people. They weren't interested in climbing any ladder; their concern was pastoral. They just had such good hearts. Bishops Gerry Wiesner and Henri Goudreault were so good at getting language that the rest of them could agree to.

The first document probably took us a year and a half to develop. It was released in October 1996 and was entitled "To the Families of the North: The Challenge of Family Healing; Part 1." A second pastoral letter, in February 1997, was entitled "Responding to Family Violence." The third message ("The Challenge of Family Healing: Part 3") was a message of hope and encouragement and was approved in July 1997.

The 1996 statement says, "…there have been misunderstandings of church teaching in this regard and many people continue to suffer because of these misunderstandings." Well, the teaching that they were referring to was that a woman had to stay in her situation, and a lot of people in the North, church people (not only Catholics), felt that the shelters that were being established in some of the communities were harming family life because the women could go there. They weren't looking at why they needed to go there and what needed to be done to address that violence. In isolated communities, where could the women go?

By going around, I was able to counter these misunderstandings, explain that none of that had ever been part of church teaching, and use the statements to show people, "See, the bishops say that's just not true." That first statement was translated into all the First Nations languages (at least 10, I think) used across those eight dioceses. The statement was read on every local community radio and in every parish in every diocese on the same Sunday. This had probably not been done ever before in Canada.

The second statement read, "Family violence is a result of unequal power and control. Victims are always those who are in some way dependent on the abuser." And later, "violence against women is a sin"... also a "social sin that is part of our families, communities and even our church." This was a huge dynamic to address. What impressed me is that the bishops understood this theological and pastoral significance of family violence and were willing to clearly state it. I was sowing seeds to try to get some of this analysis out there. The truth was in all the research I did on family violence, so that wasn't new.

Was anything done as a result? Each diocese in its own way established a project to support family life; many of them did this in terms of addressing their own marriage preparation and marriage renewal programs. I'd hope it continues to be done. It raised consciousness at least.

I personally didn't experience any pushback from the male clergy in the church. In the North there were few priests, and they were getting on in years, so they did what they could. In some communities there were lay leaders; some of them objected. Bishop Croteau was dumbfounded after one visit in his diocese when the men argued with him! They were mad as blazes with him, even arguing about Scripture! So there was more pushback in that way than from any of the priests, I would say.

The concern about violence surfaced more in my visits with Indigenous women; however, I need to say that it was present across the board. One sister, a nurse on the coast of Labrador, told me that the amount of violence in the small, isolated non-Indigenous communities she served was extraordinary. So I began to suspect that isolation had something to do with violence, as well as the downturn in the cod fishing economy. People had no idea where to go with any of that, and sexual abuse was a very big problem in small non-Indigenous communities as well.

In Yellowknife, the bishop asked the president of the Catholic Women's League to read the message on his behalf at Mass there, where there were very few Indigenous people in the congregation. I knew every word we had struggled over and reviewed. Then, when she had finished reading, there was this moment of silence, and everybody clapped, and tears ran down my cheeks…

That same person at the next CWL meeting asked the women what they thought, and one answered, "Well, we all know it was just Sr. Marie who wrote that…." But the president said, "She may have drafted it, but the bishops worked on it and they have signed it and sent it out." An older Filipino woman put up her hand and said, "I've been waiting my whole, entire life to hear the church speak out on this. It's everywhere."

Indigenous people speak more openly about what they are suffering, compared to a lot of non-Indigenous people, so who knows how this letter impacted those who tend to keep all that stuff hidden. It would be wrong to think that this was only a problem in Indigenous communities. After the statements were released, a woman contacted me from Saskatchewan, asking me to come and get her bishop to do something like this. Because, she said, violence is a big problem there, too. But I said, "No. Now you go and get to work on this issue!"

The statistics I was reading and used in the statements referred to the fact that 30 percent of Canadian women experienced at least one incident of physical or sexual violence at the hands of a marital partner. All incidents of assault are accompanied by emotional abuse. We knew that the statistics were even higher in the North. If a pastor looked out at a congregation of 500 families, then perhaps 150 were impacted by violence. Isn't that amazing? The statistics from the United Nations concerning violence against women are high (at 35 percent), but they don't even include women who have been verbally abused, or who have been financially kept in prison by men – these are also forms of violence.

Our work gave hope to some women at the time. The social agencies and people working with women were very appreciative of these statements and the work we were doing. They were trying to raise awareness, and this gave additional support to them, an affirmation from an organization that's been influential in the North. It was very important.

We know that violence against women and children continues today and that there are ways to address it, beginning with acknowledgement, progressing to providing safety for victims, addressing underlying causes, developing treatment programs for both men and women, training for police and Crown attorneys, etc. But faith communities don't seem to be following up on this issue of family violence. Although I am no longer in the North, I never hear it referred to anymore, anywhere.[1]

A questionnaire came out in preparation for the Synod on the Family (October 2015 in Rome) a couple of years ago. I was really frustrated and annoyed because all the questions were related to the sacraments and family prayer.

---

1 Earlier, the CCCB's Permanent Council published the statement "To Live Without Fear," in June 13, 1991. It condemned violence against women as *a sin, a crime, and a serious social problem*. Pastoral approaches that are helpful or harmful were listed, and proposals made for long-term prevention. On March 27, 1992, the CCCB president joined ten other church leaders before the Canadian Panel on Violence Against Women in the submission "And No One Shall Make Them Afraid." It stated that violence against women is *profoundly wrong*, described the underlying causes, acknowledged ways in which churches contribute to the problem and the solution, and made specific recommendations for church and government action.

In this larger document from Rome there was reference to families living in wartorn areas and people living in political conflict, but there was no reference to this experience of family violence. And so I sent a letter, with copies of the statements on family violence that the bishops of the North had signed and developed, to the current bishops of the North. I reminded them that their predecessors had spoken out then. And although I'm unaware of what each diocese may be doing now, I can't imagine that it's any better. I strongly encouraged them, in responding to the Synod questionnaire, to raise this issue of violence within the home. Nothing ventured, nothing gained…

I got a couple of responses. One archbishop asked me why I wouldn't send in this feedback myself. I replied that I certainly planned to do so, but that we both realize that something coming from an archbishop would have more weight than something coming from me! Another bishop responded to say that he would forward my letter to the committee working on preparation for the Synod. So I didn't get a sense that anybody would do much about it at the Synod. But Archbishop Paul-André Durocher of Gatineau, Québec, made violence against women a major theme during his intervention. (His call for the Catholic Church to be open to ordaining women as deacons received more attention from the press.)

If I had continued in the North, I would have done more follow-up. I strongly recommended that someone be hired to do some coordinated follow-up, that it not just remain in the hands of each diocese to respond. However, during that year I was named provincial of my congregation, so I moved back to Victoria. I know they did not hire another person to follow up in a coordinated way, although individual dioceses did act in various ways.

I realize that a Commission of Inquiry into the question of Missing and Murdered Aboriginal Women, which Indigenous and faith communities have called for, is now in place. As faith communities, we can support with a strong voice those communities that have been most affected and can strive to understand and address the underlying causes of such violence. I'm not sure about faith communities having input into this Commission's work, nor am I sure that faith community input would be particularly welcome.

On the other hand, when I worked with religious communities of sisters at the United Nations, through our organization, UNANIMA, we focused on the trafficking of women, which dovetails nicely with the work I'd done in the North. The work on missing and murdered Indigenous women and children ties in nicely with what I had learned – with the social bias against Indigenous people, as well as women and children, which is still evident. Society sees them as somehow expendable…

In the work that we do with each other in faith communities, we could try to educate people on the conditions that have given rise to this situation. The attitudes that remain towards women, especially towards Indigenous women, are still dismissive.

Marie Zarowny, a school principal, was appointed the first co-ordinator of the Social Justice Office of the Diocese of Victoria in 1977.

After her decade of service in the North, in 1998 Marie assumed leadership of the Sisters of Saint Ann in Victoria; she continues in this role today. She chaired a task group of Catholic dioceses and religious communities involved in Residential Schools, working with First Nations and negotiating with the federal government, and represented women religious at the historic private audience of First Nations with Pope Benedict XVI in April 2009.

Marie served on the Board of UNANIMA, an NGO at the United Nations, and in Haiti (2006–07). She holds a B.Ed., an M.A. in Theology, and two honorary doctorates.

CANADIAN CHURCHES CHALLENGE THE ECONOMIC SYSTEM

Photo by Robert Dickson

INTERVIEW WITH BILL PHIPPS

Canadian faith communities are renowned for caring for the poor. Church liturgies employ moving language to pray for those in need among us, collections of foodstuffs are offered to local food banks, and monetary contributions are directed towards local and international charities. Surveys constantly confirm that people of faith volunteer more hours, and give more in charitable donations, than the general population.

But do these good works of charity create the structural change that is so urgently needed for justice to prevail in Canadian society?

At notable times in recent history, leaders in Canadian churches have made significant attempts to move from charity to justice – challenging the population, and political leaders, to deeper reflection and action for change.

One such moment occurred in the late 1990s, under the leadership of the Moderator of the United Church of Canada, the Right Reverend Bill Phipps. Phipps wanted to initiate a process whereby thousands of individuals could engage in conversations and reflections on the burning economic issues of the day from a moral perspective. The process was marked by exciting, and new (at that time), uses of the internet to allow for wider engagement of citizens than ever before.

Early in Phipps' term of leadership, after a six-hour interview with the Ottawa Citizen, *journalist Bob Harvey reported that this leader of the nation's largest Protestant denomination questioned the divinity of Jesus. Through the resulting media storm, Phipps recognized the upside: he now had the attention of Canadians concerning his views on church and society. Phipps deftly took advantage of this moment to reinvigorate his denomination's tradition of the "Social Gospel" of economic justice, and "The Moderator's Consultation on Faith and the Economy" was born.*

When I became Moderator of the United Church in 1997, I wanted to have a theme for my time. A lot of Moderators don't do that. Most of the time, Moderators decide what they want to focus on as their time in the job goes on. But I felt very strongly that we had been through a period of years where we were doing a lot of introspection. The whole debate on the rights and place of gay and lesbian people in society was huge, and also whether ordination and commissioning was open to gay and lesbian people.

That occupied a lot of United Church energy in the 1980s, and quite rightly so. We really worked at that; it's a justice issue. But the focus was not as much on economic justice during those years. Economic justice was one of my passions throughout my ministry from the time I was ordained. Also, it was very basic to the foundation of the United Church of Canada. It's one of the things the United Church has brought to the public and to our ecumenical work. I thought the timing was right to get people to remember "the Social Gospel," to understand why it's essential to living out Christian faith – and why and how the United Church had been a leader (along with others) in that enterprise.

We produced six or seven books during that time. Among them was the Rev. Dr. Ted Reeve's[1] *Claiming the Social Passion.* On the back cover, I explained why we undertook the Moderator's Consultation. "With human dignity and ecological integrity hanging by a thread, people yearn for moral moorings to undergird our common soul. Consumerism and extreme wealth overpower citizenship and solidarity. Recognizing the fateful realities where most are excluded from social well-being, I initiated the Moderator's Consultation on Faith and the Economy." That's a good three-sentence statement about why I wanted to do it.

The Moderator's Consultation on Faith and the Economy was nothing new in terms of church teaching, but on the other hand this was really a new and exciting initiative to undertake.

The people who were engaged in the Moderator's Consultation were from different churches and different kinds of involvements. It was a Moderator's Consultation, but it wasn't a United Church project. Whoever was interested in these issues could easily become involved without thinking they had to be supporting the United Church. I think it was a fairly imaginative example of ecumenical work at that time.

In 1998 to 2000, the World Council of Churches was talking about "Justice, Peace and the Integrity of Creation." And the churches were approaching the Jubilee Year 2000 by focusing

1 Ted Reeve, *Claiming the Social Passion: The Role of the United Church of Canada in Creating a Culture of Social Well-being in Canadian Society* (Etobicoke: United Church of Canada, 1999).

on cancelling debts of poor countries and proposing structural change in society. I think these were new experiences of church. On the other hand, it wasn't new if we go back to the Social Gospel, even to the late 19th century, and all those efforts even prior to the United Church being formed in 1925.

What I mean by that is that the United Church, from its Methodist roots primarily, inherited the Social Gospel tradition. Then it found its own expressions through people like J.S. Woodsworth, and the whole cadre of people who were in the socialist camp, trying to address issues of the Great Depression and issues of war. That's what I mean by saying it's not new.

We were still involved in those things as part of our living out the gospel and our social action work, including things like the Canadian Urban Training Project. The United Church provided a lot of funding for that, and a lot of United Church ministers went through that training. We began to perceive that the market really had become God. Although the Thatcher/Reagan/Mulroney years were behind us, and those leaders were no longer in power, the Chicago School of Economics and neoliberalism had really taken hold. Social welfare and public health care were in jeopardy. Services were under pressure of privatization.

During the Moderator's Consultation, I would always talk about the market becoming God and ours becoming a hyper-consumer society. "Consumerism on steroids" is how I phrased it. In the period of the '50s, '60s, '70s and the beginning of the '80s, we had tried to maintain some sort of a balance of public welfare and the market. We sought a balance of government projects, government involvement and market solutions. But then the neoliberal economic theories really took hold – John Maynard Keynes was out and Milton Friedman was in. It wasn't just "business as usual" from a post-war perspective. Rather, we were being railroaded by market ideology. In large part, what I was trying to say from a Christian perspective was that the market is not God, and economic justice is a fundamental cornerstone of biblical theology.

Jim Wallis of *Sojourners* magazine would cut out all the mentions of economic issues in the Bible, and then he'd shake the book – and there would be nothing left! We had lost a lot of our moral moorings, and I remember that's the phrase that I used to quote. People were yearning for a morality that was at the heart of our public policy and our Christian witness.

While there were not huge, new or updated theological insights added from our Social Gospel theological tradition, the whole question of ecological integrity was moving more and more into the centre of the conversation. In the Social Gospel from the late 19th century up to the Second World War, there wasn't much thought given to Mother Earth. Whereas by the time this Consultation got going, we started to talk about it more. Our title was The Moderator's Consultation on Faith and the Economy, but for me that also included environmental questions.

In fact, in the fall of 1997 I remember going to Ottawa with Joy Kennedy (of the Anglican Church) and David Hallman (United Church staff) and giving Prime Minister Jean Chrétien our first boxes of petitions on climate change. That was among the first ecumenical efforts on climate change, undertaken by the Canadian Council of Churches as part of the World Council of Churches' support for the Kyoto Accord.

While we engaged the concerns of the Social Gospel, I recall there was not much discussion about Indigenous rights. (Although, as Moderator, in October 1998, I apologized to former students of the United Church's Residential Schools.) I doubt we dealt with that at all, but at least we were broadening the scope of the Social Gospel a little bit from economic justice to include ecological justice.

There were certainly some vigorous strategic debates. Should the church engage everyone in the whole society?

Or should we create clearly focused ginger groups to push a different economic agenda, like they had done in the 1930s in the Fellowship for a Christian Social Order (1934–1945)? United Church academics like Roger Hutchinson and Richard Allen have studied the effects such church groups had on the birth of the Canadian Commonwealth Federation (the precursor of the New Democratic Party). Should we attempt to do the liberal church thing of trying to engage and move everybody along the spectrum a little bit? Ultimately, we realized that the Moderator only has a two-and-a-half-year opportunity during a term to do broadly based education, and so we decided to focus broadly on how the Social Gospel plays out in our time.

The co-chair of our advisory committee was Walter Pitman (Pitman went on to become a member of Parliament, a member of provincial Parliament and a university president).

Rev. Ted Reeve played a key role. Ted's 2000 book *God and the Market: Steps Toward a Moral Economy* outlined what we were trying to do. Chapters were provided by folks like Mark Hathaway, (former Moderator) Bruce McLeod and Moira Hutchinson.

The Atkinson Foundation (arising from the founder of the *Toronto Star*), where Charles Pascal was director, provided $250,000 in essential funding for the Moderator's Consultation. This allowed us to cover costs for salaries, videos, booklets, etc. Charles saw a perfect fit with the Foundation's history, because Joe Atkinson was a Social Gospeller and a good friend of Moderator Roberts, back in the 1930s. Charles felt Joe Atkinson would love this project; he would love to see the United Church becoming high profile again on the Social Gospel.

Sometimes such large undertakings meet with opposition inside the church. A few of the staff at the General Council offices were not very happy with this project because we went out and raised a lot more money than some United Church programs had. We were demonstrating that there were groups who see their own agendas as compatible with the church's. And while the church doesn't have the resources we used to have to do this work, there are resources and civil society partners out there. We can seriously team up with people if we use our imaginations and look around for those people who want to share our prophetic energy and ideas.

The Consultation went on for two years. In those days, it was relatively new to have online seminars. If it wasn't for Ted Reeve, it wouldn't have happened, and Mark Hathaway served as our web administrator. As I mentioned, we also released booklets on various themes. Some examples of topics were *The Church's Witness and Calls for Action* and *Seeking a Moral Economy*. The second theme was *Canadian Issues*; theme three was *For the Common Good, Global Solidarity in Seeking Justice, Peace and the Integrity of Creation*. The fourth was *Corporate Responsibility* and the fifth was *Pushing the Boundaries of Christian Action* – and that one was 200 pages long! These were substantial materials. I look at them now and I think, "How did we ever get all that done plus all the television programs from the town halls?"

We also organized seven town halls. We had them in smaller places, often in communities like Cape Breton where the coal mines were shutting down, or Port Alberni where the logging was in trouble. Basically, we invited the community and I would be the keynote speaker and master of ceremonies. Other people from the community would then talk about their economic reality. And they were quite open and engaging.

We taped these sessions and then they played on Vision TV. We engaged the grassroots of Canada as much as we could in open meetings and then put that on television. They were great events. People responded very vigorously because people were not often invited to talk publicly about the economic pressures that communities were under.

The Consultation also tried to involve people who were highly regarded in their fields. An amazing experience to conclude the process was our public forum in the Railway Committee Room of the House of Commons.

David MacDonald (United Church minister, former Conservative MP and Cabinet minister) had all kinds of contacts and knew how to get things done there. We invited the leaders of all the parties to come and tell what their economic justice policies were and then be open to questions. Not all the leaders came, but there were representatives from every party there. I remember Deborah Grey was the lone Reform MP who came. She was great; she got right in there and was very forthright. And I remember we had a great panel with Judith Maxwell, Armine Yalnyzian, Gerry Barr and Maude Barlow, among others.

I remember Bill Blaikie (NDP MP and United Church minister) standing up and saying to Maude, "You know, you still have to get people elected. It's all well and good to have people in the street and do what you do, Maude, but unless you lobby members of Parliament who are open and have the ability to pass legislation, it can't go anywhere." I remember their friendly exchange…

As the sort of figurehead, I was able to bring people together to have that remarkable gathering. Getting that calibre of public intellectuals and members of Parliament together in a room where the citizens were setting the agenda and getting the parliamentarians to give their views was certainly a highlight. I still run into people who remember it.

The other thing was, especially during my time as Moderator, my theology really got people's attention. *The Globe and Mail* did three cartoons of me during my term. I'm the only Moderator where there was a serious petition to remove him from office because of his theology!

One of the reasons we did this Consultation was because a front-page interview with me in the *Ottawa Citizen* set off a whole chain of events. I was on the front page of papers and talk shows and it all started because of my theology. Immediately I said, "This is terrific! Let's get the Social Gospel into every conversation." I got all kinds of hate mail, but we took advantage of the moment. We had the public's attention (basically because people wanted to get me out of office or were saying I wasn't a Christian). I saw that as an opportunity to engage all kinds of people that we otherwise would not have engaged.

People would phone me up or write me letters calling me a communist, asking, "Aren't you in favour of the capitalist system which brings us jobs?" That's exactly what the prophetic voice is supposed to do: get people's reaction! That's exactly what Amos and Micah do in the Older Testament, and that's what Jesus does, too. It was a highlight for me that people could see that economic justice is a critical moral question. Not just the economists or the business people or the labour unions talking – it's a moral question. You need to engage faith communities in these discussions as well.

The United Church got much more reaction when we had the whole debate on sexuality for a decade, especially homosexuality. But by 1997 I was glad to know that people could get angry about something other than sex! (We all know people who think morality is only about sex.)

The impact of the Moderator's Consultation was far greater than I expected, considering the short time we had. The reason for having that impact was the work that Ted and others like Mark and Walter and Bruce McLeod did in the background. There was very strong support from my Moderator's Advisory Committee. I expected I would get a lot of support from the Division of Mission in Canada and World Outreach staff, but the people who really got on board were Shel Reisler, Mary Frances Denis, Kate Rod and the communications people. The media staff saw a Moderator who could communicate with the media as well as with the public, a fellow who could do the

30-second clip, and a program that was communicating with Canadians, so they quickly decided to get on board.

When I talk about the right relations work with Indigenous peoples and climate change work that I'm doing now, people say, "You're a church person. What's that got to do with these things?" I go back and talk about the Moderator's Consultation, I talk about the civil rights movement, which in the States was led in large part by the churches. Martin Luther King and his crowd were Baptist. When I studied in Chicago, the major funder of Saul Alinski's community organizing work was the Catholic archdiocese! All the churches were involved in social change!

When the churches are losing confidence that they have anything to say about anything, our lived history reminds people that we do have something essential to say in the public conversation. We can remind ourselves that the churches, and biblical theology, are relevant to the social issues of the day, and that historically, periodically, we have risen to the occasion.

Right now, in various climate change conversations and doing right relations work with Indigenous people, I always talk about spiritual questions and ethics. "Tell me more about that," they ask, because people are still yearning for moral moorings. That's what I said back then during the Consultation, and that's still true today. They are yearning for a word from the religious traditions that touches them, and makes sense, and leads to action.

It's fascinating that society is getting more of this message from the Indigenous community... at gatherings of Indigenous people they always begin with prayer. If I did that, a white Christian guy, they'd say I'm imposing colonialism! But Indigenous people would just look at you like you're an idiot if you don't open a gathering with prayer. I think it shows that what we did with the Moderator's Consultation is still relevant. People are looking for moral, ethical leadership, because they know they face moral questions that are also economic and political questions.

I would be absolutely delighted if the churches would do something like the Consultation again. The time is right. We still need the Christian biblical voice on the economy because the market is taking over and people are feeling dislocated. We are not in a dissimilar situation now. The exciting thing for me today is that a lot of these issues are being seen together. When I talk to a group and say that economic justice, Indigenous rights and climate change are all intimately connected, people get it.

I don't know where the leadership impetus or the funding would come from. It would be interesting to know if the Atkinson Foundation would want to fund this 20 years later.

When the Moderator's Consultation was completed, the Atkinson people told us we couldn't stop now, because there was an awful lot of public interest generated. So, they funded the first five years of Faith & the Common Good. In those early years, we worked on health care concerns because of the privatization push and did education about consumerism, too. Today, Faith & the Common Good's brand is an interfaith project that propels faith communities to environmental responsibility. Along with Citizens for Public Justice, I think these are the two religious groups that are doing the best work on climate change.

Ted Reeve and I are still working together on something called "Feast for the Common Good." The idea is that people come together for a nice meal and conversation on meaningful topics. Depending on which church you're doing it in, we share a three-course dinner (sometimes even with wine now!), with locally based foods as much as possible. We show a PowerPoint presentation and pose questions for each course. The idea is to allow people, in their conversations over a good meal, to see the connection of climate change, right relations and economic inequality. We've done it in Orillia and in Mississauga, and we find that people will talk more easily and get to a deeper level if it is a conversation over some nice ambience, a good, slowly paced meal, with no flip charts, no outcomes – just talking together. The evaluations in those places were very positive. People loved the slowness of the evening and that we didn't have facilitators but just waited to see what would happen. We're doing it again in Calgary and then adding a workshop the following day to pick up on what people talked about over the meal. Some fabulous 20- to 30-year-old people are organizing it, and they're using Johanna Macy's work on reconnection, which is very interesting. People are responding today once again because they see that these issues are connected – and that they are all ethical questions.

Born in Toronto, Bill Phipps graduated from the University of Toronto, Osgoode Hall Law School, and McCormick Theological Seminary (Chicago). He practised poverty law and directed Neighbourhood Learning Centres at Humber College before serving as minister at several congregations in Toronto and Calgary. For a decade, he was the executive secretary of the Alberta Northwest Conference, and from 1997 to 2000, Moderator of the United Church.

He has represented the United Church in the Philippines, East Timor, Central America, South Sudan, Israel/Palestine, Congo, and various conferences with the World Council of Churches.

Bill published Cause for Hope *in 2007. He lives in Calgary and is married to writer Carolyn Pogue. They have children and grandchildren in Yellowknife, Winnipeg and Toronto.*

CANADIAN CHURCHES DEFEND MEDICARE

Photo by Anita Brinkman

INTERVIEW WITH PETER NOTEBOOM

The public health care system is an icon in our country – something often referred to as a defining difference between Canada and our neighbour to the south. Those of us with family and friends in the US see directly how private health insurance plays a much larger role there, and how the system provides inadequate coverage for many needy people who require care.

Churches have been involved in the provision of health care services in Canada since the mid-17th century, and were in the forefront of every effort against disease that Canada has known, according to a short history published by the Canadian Council of Churches. (See Joe Gunn, "Charter and Covenant: The Churches and the Struggle for Public Health Care in Canada," in A Health Care Covenant, *Canadian Council of Churches, 2007.) People of faith believe (as Sister Nuala Kenny stated in the foreword to that document) that "A health care encounter remains a place of moral meaning for patients and their loved ones." Beyond the provision of care for the sick, however, the churches have also encouraged people of faith to act as advocates for beneficial social change by attempting to influence policies designed to improve health care systems. As a rationale for such actions for change, the churches often referred to 1 Corinthians 12:12-26: "If one member suffers, all suffer together with it ... if one member is honoured, all rejoice together with it."*

In 1947, Saskatchewan Premier Tommy Douglas, a Baptist minister, introduced universal hospital insurance in that province. Although Canadian public opinion was leaning towards the need for public medical and hospital insurance, some staunch opponents could be found among the Christian communities (for example, some in the Catholic hierarchy and some religious congregations feared government intrusion in, or the outright loss of, their hospital properties and health care ministries). By the late 1950s and early 1960s, several national church bodies passed resolutions in favour of public health insurance, or presented briefs to the Royal Commission on Health Services, chaired by Justice Emmett Hall. In June 1964, the Hall Commission report was released, calling for a universal, compulsory, tax-financed national health insurance program, as well as a wider range of health services (free dental care and eyeglasses for children, expectant mothers and those on welfare, a prescription drug plan, fluoridation of all community water systems, care for the mentally ill and tuberculosis patients, etc.). Hall's report was opposed by some major social organizations, like the Canadian Medical Association, and politicians like Alberta's Premier Ernest Manning, who scoffed, "Next you'll be proposing grocerycare!"

Into this maelstrom stepped Canadian faith communities, as they organized the first interfaith sortie of the churches into the health care debate. In November 1965, in Ottawa's Chateau Laurier hotel, 250 people spent three days discussing the health charter that Hall had proposed. The Canadian Jewish Congress, organized labour and several Christian organizations reiterated the need to support universal health coverage in Canada – which they agreed could never be delivered by private insurance schemes. Such public events and mobilizations resulted in Parliament enacting the Medical Care Act in 1968.

Nonetheless, Medicare never encompassed all the medical needs that Canadians require. Constant pressure towards privatization was felt from private insurers and groups standing to gain from the US system. It often has been a struggle to maintain care, much less improve and expand services.

A key political moment arose in the early 2000s, as the Senate proposed a study into Medicare, at the same time as Prime Minister Jean Chrétien asked former Saskatchewan Premier Roy Romanow to lead a Royal Commission on the Future of Health Care in Canada. In this chapter, Peter Noteboom recounts how several Christian churches responded together, creating the Ecumenical Health Care Network, under the auspices of the Canadian Council of Churches.

The Network had a substantial impact. The advocacy of the churches to defend and improve Medicare as a reflection of commonly held values so impressed the Commission that the first recommendation of Romanow's final report (notably entitled "Building on Values") directly echoed the churches' wording and intent. Specifically, the churches called for the federal government to develop "A Health Care Covenant for All People in Canada" undergirded by nine important principles. This effort stands as a key example of how churches, working together, can helpfully engage and influence public policies through education, advocacy and raising a united voice for beneficial change.

Several persons from different church backgrounds were concerned about the threats to Canada's health care system and began meeting in early 2000. This was the initiative of Rev. Bill Jay, the United Church representative to the Canadian Health Coalition (CHC). Jay felt that wider faith community engagement in health care challenges could benefit the public debate. He was encouraged by CHC staff members Michael McBane and Frances Arbour, who were both activists in their faith communities (McBane had worked in the Social Affairs Office of the Canadian Conference of Catholic Bishops, and Arbour, a former religious sister, had staffed the Inter-Church Committee on Human Rights in Latin America).

In March of that year, at McLeod-Stewarton United Church (his congregation in Ottawa), Bill Jay convened the first recorded session. Jay was joined by Jim Marshall, Don Junk and Peter Newbury of the United Church, Stephen Allen representing the Presbyterians, David Pfrimmer of the Evangelical Lutherans, Anne Cruickshank, Mary Rowell and Dr. John Dossetor of the Anglicans, Joe Gunn from the Catholic bishops' conference, and Jim Roche of the Catholic Health Association of Canada.

The group eventually proposed to house their work under the auspices of the Canadian Council of Churches (CCC), with Marshall and Allen (two national church staff) serving as the first co-chairs of what we called The Ecumenical Health Care Network (EHCN). How did this happen? Interested people, staff persons of churches, first discover that there is a rich vein of collaboration that is possible, and find that the time is right, and get to work on an issue. Then at some point they say, "Actually, we need a convening or backbone organization, as this is more than we can handle on our own" – and then the work kind of slides to the Council as a proposal to pick up. Now, especially if leadership people are involved, it quickly becomes the business of the Commission for Justice and Peace of the Council. And that's what happened with the EHCN.

It came to the Council because member churches had already started to think about health care, were worried about growing threats of privatization of services, and desired to invite the Council to become an organizing space for this work.

These participating representatives served as a concerned core group among the church members in the Council, but the EHCN was always open to the participation of other interested communities. Soon, through participation in the CCC, representatives of the Salvation Army (another faith community that was known for health care ministry among its constituency) joined the EHCN.

The EHCN's first public act was in 2001, when we wrote to Health Minister Allan Rock, requesting a meeting. The churches also recognized a key political opportunity for advocacy, which needed to be grasped. There was a fear that public-private partnerships or other developments in the delivery of health care services in Canada would undermine the universality of health care coverage. The Kirby Commission in the Canadian Senate was approached, and Stephen Allen (Justice Ministries staff of the Presbyterian Church in Canada) presented a brief to this Commission on behalf of the EHCN on October 29, 2001. Kirby was seen to be quite critical of the publicly funded Medicare system, so Allen forcefully argued that the Christian churches wanted integrated health strategies based on the social determinants of health, and were even in favour of expansion of services to include pharmacare and home care.

The Network also worked hard to develop a brief to the Romanow Commission. But the presenting cause for working through the CCC specifically was the need to organize a forum, the "Canadian Churches Forum on the Future of Health Care in Canada," on Parliament Hill in February of 2002. That was a huge organizing effort. Letterhead needed to come from a convening organization that could bring in the guest speakers and politicians who really needed to attend such an event, and the Council could ably do that.

There were three circles of influence at that Forum that the churches did well. It attracted really key, core denominational people; it was able to expand that by bringing in expert participants who knew the health sector really well; and thirdly, it really reached out to experts in the field who were concerned about reform in the health care field. So, there was Rob McMurtry (of the Romanow Commission), Dr. Michael Rachliss and Sr. Nuala Kenny – people who had some sympathy for a faith perspective and made that day quite valuable for people who came, including Hill people, who could see that this was serious business for faith communities.

A substantial strength was added to the efforts of the churches, not only by the expansion of membership among the churches, but by the presence and participation of related faith-based organizations (which were not churches). Jim Roche of the Catholic Health Association brought his substantial expertise on technical issues, and his own networks, as did John Dossetor, a medical professor and ethicist. This delivered an enormous boost of confidence around the table, as these leaders could also enunciate the faith components of health concerns. Jim Armstrong, a Presbyterian participant, was also a leader in the Community Care Access Centres in Ontario. Those experts from the health care sector itself strengthened the work. And at the time, KAIROS had a Canadian Social Issues team, led by Dennis Howlett, which used the EHCN's eight Fact Sheets on health issues in 17 workshops across Canada.

The basis of the brief to Romanow was developed by EHCN members who had sat around the table for some time and eventually hammered out several values, principles and starting points for health care, which we called "A Health Care Covenant for Canada." That was an enormously motivating, unifying effort, which became a concrete contribution to undergirding the whole final report of Romanow's Commission. That came out of the churches' own expertise in speaking to moral and ethical issues, being able to articulate those, again with the help of somebody like Dr. Nuala Kenny, a Catholic nun who had both medical training and a background in theology. It was fascinating to see how we could put those principles into words that could form a framework for the policy work.

A determining moment occurred in May 2002, when Janet Somerville (general secretary of the Canadian Council of Churches) joined Rev. David Pfrimmer (EHCN member representing the Evangelical Lutheran Church in Canada) in Ottawa's Chateau Laurier hotel to present the EHCN brief – with substantial effect – to the Romanow Commission. I think the prophetic ability of Janet Somerville to speak to health care issues was important. She had true passion for this work, which was a real contribution of the Council to this effort. While I was not there for their presentation, I have often heard stories of how Janet was able to speak to Mr. Romanow as a peer, and somehow touch his heart. From then on, we were a known quantity.

On the other hand, it is hard to evaluate how well the materials of the EHCN were used among CCC members, and presented to folks in the pews. The fact is, we have zero view about the inner workings of member denominations. We have no clue, really. Today, we might have some clue about how many times educational materials have been downloaded from our website, but back in those days it was not primarily a downloading system. Whether Lutherans or Presbyterians (for example) saw EHCN materials in their pews, it's hard to tell. Jim Roche used the Fact Sheets, we heard, through the Catholic health care network, especially among people who were interested in such topics as private vs. public care, the need for pharmacare, the social determinants of health, etc. But unfortunately, I have no real way of knowing how well this great information was used.

Development of the principles espoused in "A Health Care Covenant for Canada" certainly was a high-water mark for the EHCN's work. But reflecting critically now on 17 years of involvement with the Council, it is unclear to me what churches bring to the public policy debate, on whatever topic it might be – climate, poverty, health care, religious freedom, whatever. It seems to me that part of the value of this work is churches actually talking to themselves – even if they have *no* influence on the public policy debate! So, if they discover that in thinking about health care, or biotechnology, or undoing racism, there are some starting points for action, some common shared theological reflections, some points of unity, those can actually form the basis for collaboration. So, if we're a backbone/convening organization at the Council, it's probably not enough to say, "Well, we're all churches" or "We're all committed to the gospel." Well, what exactly does that look like in whatever topic area we're working on? So it has been true that in several different areas, the work of developing those shared, agreed-upon principles has formed a kind of foundation for further work. When there's debate or differences or whatever, you can go back and say, "Well, how are these theological principles informing our thinking about our contributions to this new policy challenge?"

I have thought of this work as not only a contribution to public policy debates, but primarily as a unifying force, internally, for churches. It's not that I've always been an advocate for development of these statements of principle to happen. (And it's true that they've always been drafted by other people, not just Council staff. I seem to remember that the Health Care Covenant, for example, was principally the work of David Pfrimmer, then reviewed by Joe Gunn, Jim Roche, Stephen Allen and the rest of the EHCN members.) But that process of developing common theological reflections became starting points for action together, and a foundation for future work.

And in the case of the Health Care Covenant, I think this was the only example of our work that got legs outside the internal workings of the churches – we saw Roy Romanow call his final report "Building on Values," and it clearly stated that "Canadians view Medicare as a moral enterprise, not a business venture." His first recommendation was exactly that of the churches – for the federal government to adopt a Health Care Covenant or Charter! We knew that our language had made an important contribution to that chapter of the Romanow Report (and when we later met with him, he confirmed that this was true).

So that was impressive – a real public policy win, it seems to me.

If what churches and faith communities have to offer is different – a faithful vision of the world in the future in Canada – then that's probably our expertise in public policy. What we can contribute are those values, those principles, those ways of thinking about the problem that are gospel-informed. That's a concrete contribution we can make to faith and public life generally.

Working together over the years, the EHCN helped develop a shared analytical framework among the church representatives. Besides the shared framework of the Health Covenant, and the intentional strategy of including experts from both inside and outside the churches themselves, there were other ingredients that made the group work well. One was a real attention to contemporary events, the changes occurring in the field of health care. I remember discussions on the way to and from meetings, usually held in Kingston, where we would share developments in the discussion of the Health Council for Canada, or interventions at the Supreme Court… we were always living in the details of health care reform, one way or another.

It was also notable that this was one of the pieces of ecumenical work that was not only southern Ontario focused. There was an awareness of the situation in Quebec – more so later when Bill Jay moved there. There was also consciousness of what was happening in Alberta, under Premier Ralph Klein at the time. And there was an important supporting network for EHCN work there. Each of the provincial manifestations of the issues was always somewhat different. Since health care is a provincially administered service, figuring out the federal contribution was always hard.

At another moment, I remember Jim Marshall brought in a network concerned with elder abuse. Here was a network of people working on issues to which we needed to also pay attention. We later had a session with the St. Stephen's ministries. So health care–related networks also influenced our activities, and further contributed to the debate.

The EHCN ended when political opportunities were fewer, especially as the years of the Harper government began. It was clear there was not a lot of listening going on. There wasn't really a discussion partner in government. There was also a turnover in membership – folks no longer had the capacity to devote their efforts to health care issues. Some of the churches suffered financial and staff cutbacks. At about this time, Jim Marshall retired from the United Church, Maylanne Maybee moved on from the Anglican Church, and after 2005 there was no representative from the Catholic bishops. A meeting in February 2008 decided to suspend the work of the Network, and a final celebratory gathering with prayers and a liturgical ceremony was held in September.

The Canadian Council of Churches has continued, periodically, to speak on health care concerns. In 2009, a letter was sent to the National Council of Churches in the USA, outlining how Canadian churches supported Medicare. Canadian faith communities did not want the US media's negative reporting on Canada's health care system to be used to derail the Obamacare initiative. And in 2014, after Barbara Lloyd, some United Church representatives and I attended a policy summit on health care organized in Ottawa by Citizens for Public Justice and the Dignity for All anti-poverty campaign, a letter was sent to Health Minister Rona Ambrose. We asked what plans were on hand for renewing financial commitments to the Health Accord with Canadian provinces. I then used this opportunity to resend several relevant EHCN documents to CCC members.

But health care issues are not on today's agenda for Canadian churches. Nonetheless, should a crisis situation or opportunity arise, Canadian churches are well positioned to respond, due to the work that was done by the EHCN. We can always return to these agreed-upon position statements – we would not be starting from zero. That is really important, even now that new individuals sit on the CCC's Commission for Justice and Peace – folks who were not involved directly in the EHCN back in the day.

Interestingly, in their program priorities for the next two years, 2016–2018, the Commission on Justice and Peace of the CCC has decided to step away from programmatic policy work and stepped towards theological reflection and dialogue and this task of establishing shared principles. In the past, the churches identified a particular political issue or advocacy opportunity, and then we tried to develop shared guiding principles for reflection and action on this concrete purpose, this political moment in time. I just need to live with this as a staff person and follow wherever the member denominations are… Now, the Commission is not naming those political opportunities; they're saying it's just important for us to get to know each other better again, and understand what it is that brings us together. I'm curious to know whether that will work.

Since 1999, Peter Noteboom has been the deputy general secretary and associate secretary, Justice and Peace, of the Canadian Council of Churches. In 2017, he became interim general secretary. An accomplished facilitator and adult educator, he is a senior partner of and chairs the Board of Global Learning Partners.

Peter has served on the Board of Trustees of the Christian Reformed Church in North America, and as World Renew's program manager for five years in West Africa.

He has been treasurer of the Institute of Christian Studies, served on the Board of the financing agency Oikocredit, and speaks English, French, Chinese and Dutch. Peter holds a master of arts in European Studies from the University of Leuven and a post-graduate diploma from Simon Fraser University.

WOMEN AROUND THE WORLD MARCH FOR RIGHTS

Photo by Lucie Bélanger

INTERVIEW WITH FABIEN LEBOEUF

Leading up to the Jubilee Year 2000, an international movement of women began to organize to ensure human rights for women around the world. Their key demands included the elimination of poverty and ensuring a fair distribution of the planet's wealth between rich and poor and between men and women; the elimination of violence against women; and ensuring equality between women and men.

The idea to organize the March was initiated by the Fédération des femmes du Québec following the great success of the 1995 Women's March Against Poverty in that province, and the 1996 Women's March for Bread and Roses in Canada.

The 1996 action saw three contingents of 850 women march for 10 days to demand economic justice for women. At the end of their walk, they were joined by 15,000 supporters.

In October 1998, 140 delegates from 65 countries met in Montreal to set international demands for the March and to create an International Liaison Committee. This group included two representatives from Canada. The March grew to be endorsed in 153 countries and by 4,190 organizations.

The issue of support for the March became extremely contentious among Roman Catholics. Whereas Development and Peace, the official international development agency of the Catholic Church, had financially supported international organizing efforts, some organizations and organizing committees in some countries supported abortion on demand. "Pro-life" organizations in Canada and elsewhere exerted massive pressure to prevent any Catholic person or Catholic organization from participating in any activity related to the March. Navigating the various debates became an intense activity for Catholic groups.

In a statement released on February 17, 2000, Bishop Gerry Wiesner, president of the Canadian Conference of Catholic Bishops, endorsed the March's major goals, which he viewed as in keeping with recent teachings of the bishops and the Holy See. On May 15, 2000, four Catholic organizations clarified their support for the primary goals of the March, while stating that they could not support each and every one of the 59 demands of the Canadian Women's March Committee. The bishops' conference, Development and Peace, the Canadian Religious Conference and the Catholic Women's League stated, "We believe that Canadian Catholics should not allow themselves to be shut out of the March of Women because some groups decide to press for demands that are clearly unacceptable to us."

In 2000, the huge March of Women descended on Ottawa, leaving from Hull, Quebec. At Notre Dame Cathedral in Ottawa, religious sisters and laity packed the building for Mass, celebrated by Archbishop Marcel Gervais in the presence of a couple of visiting bishops. And then the crowd moved out to the street to join the wave of women and their supporters who descended on Parliament Hill.

In February 2001, however, the World March of Women's International Organizing Committee protested US President George W. Bush's decision to reinstate a previous ban on US foreign aid to overseas programs that promoted abortion. At that point, Development and Peace took the difficult decision to dissociate itself from the World March of Women International Organizing Committee.

The controversy is explained here (in a conversation originally enjoyed in French) by the then executive director of Development and Peace, Fabien Leboeuf.

Leading up to 2000, I was the executive director of the Canadian Catholic Organization for Development and Peace (D&P).

The World March of Women was an international event, due to culminate in the year 2000. Many countries were involved. Development and Peace decided to participate for several reasons. The primary reason was the importance of the issues at that time surrounding the poverty of women and the human rights of women. There was no one poorer in the world than an African woman peasant farmer or an Indigenous woman, or poor women living in slums. They are not only the poorest people, but also the most oppressed. It was therefore a fundamental issue for development organizations – to promote women's rights and improve their conditions. It was not only an issue that couldn't be avoided; the poverty and oppression of women was the greatest development challenge.

At D&P, this issue was a priority. So, it was unimaginable that D&P would not get involved. The mission of D&P was not only to promote the integral development of people, defined by, for example, Pope Paul VI in his 1967 encyclical, "On the Development of Peoples." But also, we needed to engage in the struggles of the poor. Structural changes never come from those who are profiting from the status quo. Profound structural change always comes from the victims who organize themselves. So it was not possible for D&P to refuse to engage due to our Catholic commitment to justice – and it was impossible to ignore these victims of injustice.

Since the Second Vatican Council, it had become clear that Christian engagement in the struggle for liberation against oppression was a constitutive element of living the gospel. D&P, because of its mission and the social teaching of the church, had to be engaged.

We also saw that we could provide several forms of assistance that would contribute and strengthen the World March of Women. First, through the D&P network of southern partners we had financed, we had partners in thousands of base organizations, many of which were women's organizations. In many different sectors, not only Catholic or Christian groups – for D&P also supported secular organizations – we were able to assist in mobilizing these partners to participate in the March in various countries of the South.

D&P gave an initial contribution of $50,000 to the international organizing committee of the March. This was the largest financial contribution of any Canadian NGO. This helped them to carry out their organizing efforts, but we also supported many women's organizations in Southern countries, so they could organize their own participation and effective work in the March.

D&P's financial assistance was not limited to the $50,000 we gave to the secretariat to do the international organizing. We also used our education budget in Canada to mobilize our Canadian networks so they could participate. We produced educational materials on the International March of Women.

This was used for the education of the general public, as well as for the mobilization of Canadian women. We also invited the members of NGO consortia like CIDSE [the international Catholic network of NGOs] to get involved in the March.

The way the March was organized, it was possible for any and all Catholic organizations to get involved without contradicting any of the church's teachings.

The primary contribution we were able to make was to broaden and diversify the networks of D&P associates that brought important support to the March. The second contribution was our major financial support.

It was also notable that in February of 2000, a joint message by D&P, the Canadian Conference of Catholic Bishops, the Canadian Religious Conference (all the religious congregations of priests and nuns) and the Catholic Women's League was released, stating their support for March-related events to begin on March 8, 2000, International Women's Day, and ending on October 17, the International Day to Eradicate Poverty. On May 15, the four organizations released a joint statement of clarification stating that the world demands of the March contained no reference to abortion. The Canadian Women's March committee released a document with 59 demands, which the four Catholic organizations were not able to sign or support. This was a moment of substantial debate, disagreement and pressure within the Catholic community.

The international campaign had advocacy demands, but none of them related to reproductive rights [abortion] or sexual orientation, particularly when it concerned lesbians. D&P and a wide range of Catholic organizations supported that platform. On the side, there was a second document that promoted and defended all reproductive rights, comprising the right to abortion and the question of lesbianism. The groups supporting the March were asked to sign the two documents. D&P did not sign the second text.

There is a way that countries in the UN system, including the Vatican, can support declarations even if they do not agree with all of the clauses [they abstain and state their reservations]. This has long been the practice of the church. What is at stake for the church in these processes is the opportunity to participate and to influence. We cannot influence if we are not present. Because D&P assisted several groups in the South to participate in the coordinating committee sessions, these women had the opportunity to influence the larger declaration. On the international level, there were non-Catholic and Muslim groups of women who said they could not participate in the March if they were forced to adopt these positions on abortion and the rights of lesbians. It was a very painful discussion; some women's groups said that if they returned to their countries with this position on lesbianism, they would be putting themselves in danger. That's the reason why this situation of the two declarations arose. It would have been difficult for a number of women to support all the demands from Canadian women's groups in certain countries in the Global South.

The international committee did not want to expose women to the threat of violence at the hands of extremists upon their return to their countries.

I think it is really important to understand the controversy, because in February 2001, D&P withdrew its support for the March – not because of the international committee, but because of the organizing committee in Montreal. President Bush banned US foreign aid to overseas groups that promoted abortion [which was then denounced by the Canadian committee]. D&P had to withdraw its support for the March because it could not disassociate itself from the moral position of the Catholic Church. D&P has not only the right, but the obligation, to put into practice the social teaching of the church. Someone who is not in agreement with the social teaching of the church should not be in D&P (even though we know there are some bishops who do not support all the social justice teachings of the church). This was precisely the moment D&P withdrew support for the March – and precisely on this issue. Many women's organizations condemned D&P for it. Many Catholic groups criticized D&P for its lack of courage. These women did not recognize the courage that D&P exhibited in being the first organization that funded the international committee to allow the March to organize in the first place.

A lot of organizations in Canada might have supported the goals of the March, but could not finance it with substantial amounts of money.

There was enormous pressure on D&P from pro-life groups and a pro-life website (LifeSite News), as well as a few bishops who were not in agreement with the decision of the bishops' conference and D&P to support the March. It is important to say that the bishops' conference always supported D&P in this matter. (It would be wrong to say the bishops did not provide support; it was just a few who were opposed.)

The Toronto Archdiocese held back its collection for D&P as a sign of its disapproval. Their intent was to ensure that no portion of their monies would go to the March. Six or seven bishops publicly supported D&P. The majority of bishops supported D&P, but what I always find troubling is that the majority were silent. This silent majority exists among the bishops as it does among Canadian society and in any organization. I would like to honour the general secretary of the CCCB, Peter Schonenbach, who always strongly supported D&P. I was in constant contact with him concerning developments in the March so he was always aware of what was going on. Even afterwards, when bishops and LifeSite News denounced D&P, he still supported us. I was also in touch with the director of LifeSite News, to explain to him that which I've argued here. I told him that there was no reference to reproductive rights, abortion or lesbian rights in the international declaration, and explained to him the influence D&P had in the development of these positions and how important it was for Catholic organizations to be involved in women's struggles. I also told him it would be impossible to influence these debates without being present. He didn't respond to my arguments, but said that because we had associated with radical feminist groups, LifeSite was going to continue to denounce D&P. In other words, he argued in favour of guilt by association.

It is the same as what they did a few years ago with a Mexican Jesuit priest. The Centro Miguel PRO participated in a human rights consortium where other participants were feminist organizations that defended pro-choice positions. (The Mexican Jesuit was forced to end his Canadian speaking tour, and the group's funding from D&P was cut.)

For me this is a fundamental issue. We are seeing a notable retreat from the positions of Vatican II and the social teaching of the church. I think of the situation of Moses and Joshua in the Old Testament. Moses went up the mountain and defended the precepts given by God. But when he descended to the people, he saw them being unfaithful by worshipping a golden calf. Meanwhile, Joshua, whom Moses had appointed to direct the people, was involved in the day-to-day business of leading them to the Promised Land. He had to make difficult compromises and alliances. He lived in a river of tumult.

Sometimes it's easier to be Moses – it is a lot more difficult to be Joshua. Groups like LifeSite News speak moral commandments from a distance. Meanwhile, people who are in the public square defending and promoting the dignity of the human person are necessarily in contact with other groups and other people. According to the Moseses of the world, they don't have a right to be there, because they might be in contact with other associations. They fall into a sinful situation, they don't remain true to the church, and they are not true Christians. There are people who try to manipulate the church for non-Christian ends. With this kind of approach, it is impossible for a Catholic to get involved in daily struggles. In that case it is impossible to be a Catholic, with others, in the world.

Another challenge is to know what the relationship is between faith, moral thinking and being in the world. Groups like LifeSite News argue that they're in favour of women's rights, but rarely denounce torture or the bombing of civilians by the American Air Force. They would never have denounced dictatorships like Pinochet's in Chile, or any other dictator of the day.

When I was the associate general secretary of the Quebec Assembly of Bishops, I dared to say that in matters of sexuality and marriage, the church is in need of therapy. The problem is not moral, and it is not theological. It is a problem of mental health. Collective therapy is needed in the church around sexuality. In my opinion, it is a task that goes beyond D&P alone. The taboo of the discussion of sexuality in the church has become an obstacle for church organizations that need to participate in humanity's struggles for justice and human rights.

We learned several great lessons from the International Women's March. The first lesson I learned from the March is that we have to pay attention to history. People in Canada should ask where their quality of life has come from. Who struggled for the quality of life that they enjoy today? Who opposed the struggles for a better quality of life? It is imperative to situate the current reality in at least the last 200 years of history. Trade unions have struggled for years for the right to not only line their pockets, but for the dignity of the human person. People have struggled to create the quality of life we have today, and sometimes with great sacrifice, even at the cost of their lives. And having this historical perspective, people can position themselves to better understand what's going on today. Do they wish to contribute to those ongoing struggles for justice, or would they prefer to succeed in the American dream in the consumer-driven and individualistic society of today, without concerning themselves with anything else?

There is a fundamental choice to make. To involve ourselves in the struggle for dignity, justice for women, and solidarity with the struggles of poor people is a way of living and being human. I would ask people to reflect on what kind of world we would like to build for our grandkids. Would you like your daughter to live in the same situation as your grandmother? It's not only women's struggles that haven't achieved their objective, but other struggles as well.

Would you be able to pay for medical care for someone in your family if you did not have access to a public health system? The attraction of a consumer society is very powerful. For people to have another perspective on life, it's really important to understand the history and stories of older people, taught through the school system. That's why Indigenous people are demanding that their stories be told in all history lessons. History should be about the stories of social struggles and human progress.

But today, history is about elites, generals and kings, the construction of castles, the history of prime ministers and political parties. But it is not the popular stories of the people, stories of struggle for human dignity. If people don't involve themselves in this ongoing history of social struggle, they can still be very generous, and they can participate in the cycle of charitable giving that churches offer. But D&P can also be a place of learning and formation in social change.

Concerning the situation of women, even though I'm speaking as a man, I think the structure of oppression remains in place. If we look at the world, or Canada, or Quebec, we see that the mental structures of oppression are still in place. Political, economic and church structures continue to be patriarchal. In my opinion, the moral opinion of the church concerning women and sexuality reflects nothing more than patriarchal structures in the church. The church is dominated by these patriarchal structures that are thousands of years old.

Society and the churches need to disassemble these harmful structures.

Recently, I saw a cartoon in a European newspaper concerning the recent Synod on the Family, held in the Vatican. There was no commentary, just a photo of all these old men, bishops and cardinals in red robes, sitting in rows, deciding what families should do. It was a stunning illustration of patriarchy in the church today.

In 2016, the Young Liberals of Quebec convention debated a motion to establish a minimum number of female candidates for the next provincial election. A proposal to establish a quota parity of 50% female candidates was defeated. Why? The counterargument was that "individual rights" be respected. Individual rights were preferred, rather than setting a collective target. Even Young Liberals, discussing rights of women, couldn't come to an agreement. So for me, the struggle for women's rights is a long way from being realized. The structural foundation for discrimination and the structural oppression of women is still there. In the church, many declarations echo this patriarchal oppression.

Did D&P change after this experience of support for the Women's March? I don't really see how it changed in a fundamental way. Not only on paper, but in what was done. Although two things perhaps have changed that strike me today…

One is the weakened knowledge of Catholic Social Teaching and of church structures among the staff of D&P. Second, there is a greater difficulty of dialogue with the Canadian Catholic bishops. There isn't sufficient theological, intellectual and ecclesial knowledge to accomplish this inside D&P. This is a notable weakness. And that's why the bishops moved in 2010–2011 to change their mechanism of supervision of D&P. I don't think it was exclusively because of issues of women's rights. I think it's because the bishops noted a certain lack of direction in D&P.

D&P was always a place of faithful political engagement in the church. To navigate correctly in church and society, two eyes are needed. You need to understand politics and you need to understand your faith. There has been a weakness in the management of D&P to be able to look at the world with these two eyes. I hope that the next director does not repeat the mistakes of the past.

There has also been a problem in the annual collection of funds for the organization's activities. While professional fundraisers have been brought in to design these collections, they know nothing of development, the church, or where and what is "the heart of D&P." So these campaigns, experienced by millions of donors in the pews every year, do little to add to the education, and thus the commitment, of Canadians, or the Canadian bishops, to international development and solidarity. They lack a sense of supporting the organized struggles of the poor for justice – which is what D&P is all about.

Fabien Leboeuf worked for Development and Peace for over 25 years: as co-ordinator of Public Engagement Programs in Canada; as director of International Programs; and then as executive director from 1996 to 2001.

He studied in Montreal, Ottawa and France, receiving a Ph.D. in Theology from the University of Strasbourg, and a master's in International Management from the National School of Public Administration. He served as assistant executive director of the Quebec Assembly of Bishops in the 1970s, was Quebec's representative on the Inter-Church Project on Population, and was a founding Board member of KAIROS.

Fabien has served on a wide range of boards, including the first educational daycare centre in Quebec, the Company of Young Canadians, the North-South Institute, the Canadian Adult Education Institute, and as president of Quebec's Human Rights League.

CEJI MOBILIZES TO CANCEL THE DEBTS OF GLOBAL SOUTH COUNTRIES

Photo by Milan Ilnyckyj

INTERVIEW WITH JENNIFER HENRY

Canadian churches and ecumenical organizations organized a three-year ecumenical justice campaign in advance of the Jubilee Year 2000. During the first year of the Canadian Ecumenical Jubilee Initiative (CEJI), massive mobilization efforts garnered 640,000 signatures on a petition to cancel the debts of countries of the Global South. At the time, this may have been the largest petition in Canadian history.

CEJI notably opposed structural adjustment programs offered by international financial institutions. The carrot of debt relief was offered by the World Bank and International Monetary Fund along with the stick of structural adjustment, demanding the privatization of public enterprises, deregulated prices and labour markets, and the forced opening of borders to foreign investment and "free" trade. Thus, debtor governments could remain enthralled to the wealthy North. CEJI's opposition to "odious debts" (contracted by despotic regimes or through fraudulent purposes) and "ecological debts" also allowed analysis of the debt question to challenge the very structures of international underdevelopment.

In the second year of CEJI's work, several campaigns were initiated. In one notable action, coinciding with the 10th anniversary of Parliament's unanimous resolution to end child poverty in Canada, a further 60,000 petitions were gathered, demanding that politicians keep their word. The third year saw activity on Indigenous land rights (over 50,000 petitions gathered) as well as another 40,000 signatures supporting the Kyoto Protocol on climate change.

As a staff person with the Ecumenical Coalition for Economic Justice, Jennifer Henry became a member of the CEJI Steering Committee, which met weekly to advance campaign activities. Here she shares several memories, and lessons learned, from the mobilization success of the CEJI experience.

We began thinking about our possible role in organizing Jubilee campaigns in 1997. There was a petition that was beginning to circulate out of Britain. Organizationally, it wasn't getting traction – it was moving among specific grassroots folks around the question of debt cancellation. Some global partners were beginning to be involved in this campaign and were asking what our response was. There had been a papal statement (*Tertio Millennio Adveniente*, November 1994) about the Jubilee Year and debt cancellation, so that was also a contributing factor.

Ecumenical coalitions like the Ecumenical Coalition for Economic Justice (ECEJ), the Inter-Church Committee on

Africa (ICCAF) and others already had a history of working on debt, so that wasn't a new issue for us. We already had some expertise, through the Building a Moral Economy Project, where we equipped people with the capacity to respond to economic questions. Some cross-coalition work had been done even a little bit further back, preparing for the G8 meeting in Halifax in June 1995. Different coalitions had then developed a joint program of education/action in Canada and brought Southern voices into that meeting.

So when this Millennium moment arrived, it represented a focus and an opportunity to do some more things together. We started what came to be known as the Canadian Ecumenical Jubilee Initiative (CEJI). Several ecumenical coalition staff, national church staff and church agency staff began to work together. I recall that Development and Peace had already made decisions about its focus for education campaigning, but then changed that to take on the debt cancellation petition we developed in CEJI's first year.

Our first area of significant impact was the number of signatures on the debt petition: 640,000. This was a huge number on a Canadian petition, particularly one of this complexity. I really don't know if there had ever been a larger one, and within the international debt cancellation movement, the Canadian number was significant. We had more signatures than the US.

So that was key. But going hand in hand with that was the fact that we did policy work on debt issues. We were involved in policy engagement and discussion with the federal Finance Department on a regular basis. So, married with grassroots engagement was a sophisticated economic policy contribution. I remember the Finance Minister's bureaucrats would call and ask us for information, or ask us to make sense of something, because they knew we were following this issue so intensely that we had the material at our fingertips. This was the incredible work of (ECEJ researcher) John Dillon and (ICCAF staffer)

John Mihevc. There was grassroots engagement, but there was also the policy expertise and then there was actual lobbying.

A famous story came from Finance Minister Paul Martin himself, who said that he couldn't go into a church in Canada during that period without being buttonholed about the debt issue. What was striking about that was that the Finance Minister in Britain was experiencing the same thing. They would show up at the G8 meetings together with this collective pressure. And so what happened, due to this combination of lobbying, policy analysis and grassroots engagement, was that we got 100% bilateral debt cancellation from Canada, and we moved some benchmarks globally.

At that policy level, the most significant thing about the Canadian initiative was that we didn't accept the petition as it was presented to us from colleagues in other parts of the world. Their petition had more limited language around debt "relief", which we shifted to debt "cancellation." It was also significant that we developed the language for our petition in consultation with colleagues from Quebec, thus ensuring it had a larger appeal. And we added the line about reducing structural adjustment conditionality. Our perception was that if there was only debt relief and it continued with structural adjustment conditionality, then that just wasn't sufficient change, and that in fact the situation might be exacerbated.

We were advised in many ways against this. It made the petition much more robust and it required people to understand the shift from essentially a charity position to a justice position. We persevered. I would say, again, the insight of John Dillon helped us to understand this, because he heard our partners' voices. They were really clear that that was the critical question. And we did make some progress on that question of lightening structural adjustment conditionality – it began to be something that our Finance Minister was advocating in the broader G8 process.

We could never have expected the response that we received, either in terms of the engagement of people or in terms of our impact on policy and our contribution to the global movement. Ecumenically, we have only been able to achieve the kind of strength in numbers in such a large-scale initiative when the Roman Catholic Church and the Protestant churches are on the same page. That's a deeper sense of the Christian community, right? So the reality is that in the first year of the Initiative, Development and Peace, and the Roman Catholic Church itself operating under essentially a papal mandate, put the debt question right out to the people in the pews. That we generated those kinds of numbers, both in the Francophone and Anglophone, Roman Catholic and Protestant communities, was transformative. We saw this again in the opposition to the Iraq War in 2003, and in 2005 when we came together again on the bottled water campaign.

But it wasn't like you could do this petition anytime. It had what we would call a *kairos* moment attached to it. It was a particular call, at a particular time, which was made from deep into the tradition, but made contemporary sense.

Another highlight was the development of a collaborative constituency approach in theological reflection. We developed a Vision Statement that was not drafted by a couple of theologians working alone in a room, but through a collaborative process of theologians, activists and educators. Our Vision Statement made a direct connection between praxis, theological reflection and then action. And there were three theological conferences and we published three books, lifting up these questions with significant collaboration among Quebec folks. Not only were they engaged politically through Development and Peace, but a Quebec Jubilee group emerged, and that organization has continued (in a changed form). To a certain extent, those relationships have continued.

I would say that there was also a deepening commitment to social justice inside organized churches. Because CEJI's work was framed biblically, because there was theological reflection, because it was global (and many of the churches were being called to participate globally by their global counterparts), CEJI broke through the engagement by only seasoned social justice activists, to the people in the pews. That was because there were many different entry points. You could participate on the debt cancellation petition, but you could also do theological reflection on Jubilee. You could come in by offering expressions of art, and you could come in through an exploration of eco-spirituality, or through an exploration of right relationships with Indigenous peoples. These multiple entry points offered the opportunity for the kind of folks who might not be engaged in the policy or political questions, to become engaged – to make quilts, to write poetry, to compose music. There were many ways to respond, and so there were many more responses.

In the global context, Jubilee efforts were mostly campaigns for debt relief. In Canada it was an initiative that included theological reflection, education and political action, and it was not only on debt issues but on a host of issues that were inspired by our interpretation of the biblical text in a Canadian contextual way. So the Canadian experience of Jubilee was unique, and helped build the connections with other places that shared an interest in a fuller, more transformative process.

We decided that the three-year themes of the Initiative were going to be 1) release from debt, 2) distribution of wealth and 3) renewal of the earth. The action related to the first theme was relatively clear: a debt cancellation petition in concert with the global petition. In the second year, we were challenged by the success of the first year. People wanted their specific issues included. Because redistribution of wealth was a broad theme, many actions were included as we attempted to keep people engaged. Maybe folks felt overwhelmed in that second year by the number of actions that were possible. No one action had anywhere near the strength of the debt action, which we had been able to achieve on the basis of unity.

In the third year, we had a compromise position. There were two focal areas: one around ecological justice and climate questions, and the other around Indigenous rights and land claim questions, both North and South. So there was a more focused set of issues in the third year. The critical thing was strong attempts to try and integrate local and global analysis and bridge economic justice and ecological justice.

One of the challenges of CEJI was the issue of biblical interpretation. We took a positive look at the Jubilee text in the Vision Statement and in the early theological books. Our tendency was to try and inspire the renewal of commitment and actions for social change. As time went on, we heard from folks who had different readings of those texts. Other parts of the Levitical texts are challenging – they could be understood as contrary to justice and human rights, and maybe we weren't looking at this part of Leviticus critically enough. So we produced subsequent work to "engender Jubilee." These reflections were on gender and women's rights as related to the Jubilee Initiative, and then a further piece around Indigenous perspective. The Indigenous Theological Forum was an attempt to respond to folks who felt that those perspectives were not well reflected in the early years' material. So, importantly, that criticism led us to deeper reflection.

I think it was a fair criticism that we may not have sufficiently acknowledged the racism, the religious intolerance, the homophobia and patriarchy that was in and around the book of Leviticus itself. Leviticus is a very strong text used against LGBTQ people. And yet that wasn't an issue that we were able to engage on, even though it is clearly a justice question. We were challenged to ask what a Jubilee for the churches would actually look like if the focus was more internal. Not just doing justice, but *being* just. I don't think we were able to address that as strongly as we might have.

Some of the limits had to do with the representation and the diversities within the participant communities, but some of it also had to do with organizational positions. Where people engage individually, at a local level, for example, sometimes more radicalism is able to be present, because they aren't mediating organizational challenges. In the end, we did together that which we could do together, and left aside those things that continue to separate us until this day.

As a faith-based movement, we could give leadership within the broader social movements. I went to Cologne in June 1999 to present the petition as part of the G8 Initiative. There was a lot of excitement in the Canadian press, but what was achieved in Cologne by the G8 was very modest in terms of actual change. The question of structural adjustment conditionality was still on the table. I was doing press work for the Initiative and I remember a phone call with some of the communications staff of the churches: their message was that we needed to sound positive because so many people had been involved in the debt petition. They needed to feel that they had accomplished something that was real and meaningful. On the other hand, I was with some of our Southern partners who were saying that these were "not just crumbs – they were poisoned crumbs." I remember that quote. From the Southern perspective, if the G8 didn't end structural adjustment conditionality, it wasn't a solution. The G8 was refusing to address the heart of the systemic power imbalances that existed to control Southern economies externally.

In face of these tensions, we made a good, strong decision. We got out of the way. We brought forward those more radical voices that were coming from the South, the folks saying that reparation for colonization and slavery was needed. We heard those saying we needed to address the ecological debt that the North owes the South, and to address the gender debt. In the second year and going forward, we created opportunities for those voices to speak directly to church folks in Canada. We tried to stop being a buffer in the middle.

I remember hearing from my mom, a "church lady" in a congregation in southern Ontario, when there was an announcement about the debt issue. She called and said, "So we've had another step forward on this question." I said, "Yes," and she said, "But it didn't sound like it came with any end to structural adjustment conditionality, Jennifer." And I said, "No, it didn't, Mum." And she said, "Well, we'll have to keep working." So, people judged that the folks in the South who were the most affected had to say whether what we were seeking was actually accomplished. And if we enabled those voices to speak directly to communities in Canada then they would experience the same fidelity to those communities that we staffers were striving to fulfil in that middle role.

The Canadian campaign became an ally to a growing network of Southern-based campaigns that came to be called Jubilee South. These campaigns were trying to articulate the goals and the benchmarks of the broader global movement. They resisted the control of the North, in particular the very strong British campaign. There were South African, Argentinian, Philippine, and Nicaraguan campaigns. We were influential in providing support (including financial support) to enable them to meet with each other and to magnify their voices particularly vis-à-vis the campaigns of the North (which were quite focused on a more charitable framework).

It was significant that we were able to bring Indigenous rights questions into CEJI's third year. That was the first time we had all the partners in the Jubilee Initiative focused on Indigenous rights. We had that wonderful moment, in June 2001, when we were able to spread out a thousand blankets on the lawn of the Supreme Court in Ottawa. We had Indigenous Philippine partners there, doing a Butterfly Dance. We were able to engage in solidarity with civil society organizations and national Indigenous organizations. Interestingly, we were never able to find anyone in government to accept the petition signatures that we gathered at that time. It's a testimony to how marginalized Indigenous questions were.

That was certainly a new beginning in the ecumenical commitment to Indigenous rights solidarity. In 2013, KAIROS recreated that moment, in a slightly different way. Instead of trains from across the country coming with blankets to the Supreme Court, it was banners from across the country coming to Victoria Island, to the Human Rights monument, to Parliament Hill, showing our support for the UN Declaration on the Rights of Indigenous Peoples. That kind of engagement had a new beginning there, from 2001, around the Jubilee Initiative.

There is something very powerful about this notion of a very old hymn, if you want to put it that way, which we were hearing again, anew. Each of us could find our own notes within that broader song. So we learned to sing a hymn together in a new way, but one that was sort of old and vaguely familiar. I think that was the experience for a number of us who were involved in CEJI. It was intense; we were interpersonally transformed by the experience. The irony was that we were working so hard on something that had this "rest" and "Sabbath" focus, while killing ourselves with work for the Jubilee Initiative! But for those of us for whom faith is a critical part of our activism, it was an opportunity to put things together in a fresh way and to do it in community. For the "believers" it really was personally transformative. The connections that Steering Committee members developed at our weekly meetings remain a pretty strong bond from the experience of working together in CEJI.

The work done together around CEJI certainly influenced the creation of KAIROS in 2001. There was a sense created of what we could accomplish together. Previously, there had only been a sense of the losses of coming together, forced by the restructuring of some churches. When we got to the moment of the coalition restructuring it allowed us to be not just pushed but pulled by a vision of something positive that could be the spirit of what we were going to be about.

In my view, the spirit of the Jubilee Initiative and many of the ways of working together have lived on in KAIROS. You know, we can't recreate that global context, right? And we can't recreate that particular political moment in time, which was that millennial focus. But what we have tried to do is to be faithful to things we learned about how to be and work together. For example, just a small thing, but up on our KAIROS website you will see spirited reflections. These are attempts on a weekly basis for people in our community to reflect theologically on the work that we are doing. Previously, there was a sense that theology was potentially divisive. Today, that is integrated. Maybe not in the same way, or with the same kind of focus, but even as we are engaged in social justice, we are now reflecting theologically on how that helps us.

A commitment to multiple entry points, bringing together local and global, bringing together not just ecological and economic but now also human rights in an integrated vision, that's still a part of who we are. We don't try to recreate that CEJI moment, but KAIROS now tries to draw from past insights that are helpful for the work going forward. What we are trying to do is to be attentive to what is our moment.

Now with respect to Indigenous Rights, we have another moment, where there are not 640,000 petition signatures, but there are thousands of KAIROS Blanket Exercises – so many we can't count: we can't keep up! Today, every day, new people want to embrace this. We're responding to people who are hungry for an understanding of the history of colonization and what it means in terms of injustice in the present, who want to learn and who want to be part of transformation. It's our best hope that we are of service to that transformative moment that's happening to us as a country, today, as we recognize truth and seek reconciliation.

Jennifer was raised on Treaty 1 territory in Winnipeg in the Anglican tradition. She completed bachelor's degrees of Arts and Social Work from the University of Manitoba and an MSW from the University of Toronto. Jennifer joined the Ecumenical Coalition for Economic Justice (ECEJ) in 1993 as a popular education coordinator.

After KAIROS was formed in 2001, Jennifer joined the management team, and in 2012, became executive director. She serves on the Good Jobs Roundtable of Unifor, the Board of the Centre and Library for the Bible and Social Justice, and is a member of the Primate's Commission on the Doctrine of Discovery, Reconciliation, and Justice. In 2017, she received the Anglican Award of Merit. She worships at the Church of the Holy Trinity with her partner and child.

PART 2

WHERE WE GO FROM HERE

PUBLIC MULTIFAITHISM IN CANADA AT 150

Photo by Mirko Petricevic

DAVID PFRIMMER

Søren Kierkegaard is reported to have said, "Life can only be understood backwards, but it must be lived forwards." Remembering forward is what is needed today as we think about our ecumenical past and look to our multifaith future. Historically, there have been two approaches to ecumenical work. One is *pastoral ecumenism*, with attention to dialogue and building formal relationships within and among the churches. The other is *public ecumenism*, with attention to engaging the wider public arena and the challenges facing our society. Canadian churches have made a real difference when their leaders commit to a *public theology* to be *public churches* engaging in *public ecumenism*. But Canada is changing. Public ecumenism is transitioning to what I will call *public multifaithism* with the aim of caring for Canada.

CANADIAN *PASTORAL* ECUMENISM

Pastoral ecumenism is about developing a *modus vivendi* for our faith communities *to live together* in various institutional organizations. A pastoral approach is about confidence building, establishing trust, fostering understanding and healing previous divisions in order to develop new relationships. Pastoral ecumenism involves theological dialogues, conversations, meetings, conferences and capturing agreement in published joint statements, convergence reports and theological declarations. In short, pastoral ecumenism is about how denominations *accompany* one another to expand the unity of the ecumenical family.[1]

The origins of modern ecumenism can be found in the latter half of the 20th century as churches began the processes of establishing ecumenical institutions. The two ecumenical streams of *Faith and Order* and *Life and Work* have shaped the institutional contours of 20th-century ecumenism. Pastoral ecumenism has its roots in the Faith and Order movement born at the 1910 Edinburgh Missionary Conference, eventually becoming a commission within the World Council of Churches (WCC). Pastoral ecumenism is about healing the various divisions and tidying up the unfinished business arising from the 16th-century Reformation. Faith and Order has brought churches closer together. However, pastoral ecumenism has also been a sanctuary to which the churches have retreated when they are reluctant to venture out into the more turbulent, pluralistic, diverse and contested public space – what I have de-

1 The term "ecumenism" is used to describe the building of relationships between churches in endeavouring to give visible expression to their unity as the body of Christ. The term "interfaith" or "multifaith" is used to describe relationships between faith groups more broadly.

scribed elsewhere as the "public commons."[2] A problem arises for churches when *pastoral ecumenism* dominates ecumenical life, and the public engagement of the faith communities that has shaped Canada is neglected or dismissed.

CANADIAN *PUBLIC* ECUMENISM

Historically in Canada, the more compelling ecumenical model is what I call public ecumenism. Public ecumenism traces its roots to the Life and Work movement. Even before the First World War there was "the idea of forming a worldwide movement to work for peace and justice."[3] After the "war to end all wars," church representatives began the search for a lasting peace; they eventually convened the Stockholm Conference in 1925 to articulate their plans.

Their optimism and idealism, however, were eclipsed during the early 1930s with the rise of totalitarianism and Nazism. As the Oxford conference was being planned for 1937, a new theological approach emerged that enlisted some of the great theological minds of the time and took on some of the pressing theological and ethical dilemmas. Reinhold Niebuhr summed up this direction: "It is a dangerous theology… which does not recognize how dialectically the kingdom of God is related to a sinful world in every moment of existence, offering both judgment and a more excellent way in considering every problem of justice."[4]

Public ecumenism has been hugely important to the development of Canada, to the well-being of people and the building of communities. It has involved denominations as well as agencies, theologians as well as activists, and religious

2 David G. A. Pfrimmer, "Public Ethics as a Canadian 'Theologica Publica,'" *Consensus* Vol. 36, no. 2 (2015), Article 1: http://scholars.wlu.ca/consensus/vol36/iss2/1.

3 Nicolas Lossky, ed., *Dictionary of the Ecumenical Movement*, 2nd ed. (Geneva: WCC Publications, 2002), 691.

4 Ibid., 692.

leaders as well as laity. What distinguished the Life and Work movement was its commitment to living out a Christian way of life. Whereas Faith and Order began with *believing* into a new way of *acting*, Life and Work began with *acting* into this new way of *believing* as Christians.

Canada is different today. According to sociologist Reginald Bibby, "We awake today, not to a secularized Canada, but to a polarized Canada" between religious and non-religious.[5] Canada is also polarized in its fragmented sense of *the* public. There probably never was just one public, but many diverse, conflicted and overlapping publics. In a post-Christendom time when churches have been disestablished and when the country seems fragmented, public ecumenism's challenge is to help Canadians understand the world and reimagine new publics (those associations of people, movements, organizations and institutions that help them work together), allowing us to create a more just and compassionate world. Public ecumenism draws its vitality and direction for this task from a variety of *public theologies* grounded in an authentic Christian witness to a future based upon solidarity, peace and justice.

PUBLIC THEOLOGY?

What do we mean by *public theology*? The idea originated during the 1970s. The historian of religion Martin Marty had been writing for some time about the public church and public religion. He first used the term *public theology* as he wrestled with Reinhold Niebuhr's concept of Christian realism in the American experience.[6] Jürgen Moltmann offers the following definition of public theology:

5 Reginald Wayne Bibby, *A New Day: The Resilience & Restructuring of Religion in Canada* (Lethbridge: Project Canada Books, 2012), 11.

6 Max L. Stackhouse, "Civil Religion, Political Theology and Public Theology: What's the Difference?" *Political Theology* Vol. 5, no. 3 (2004): 283, doi:10.1558/poth.5.3.275.36715.

> Its subject alone makes Christian Theology a *theologia publica*, a public theology. It gets involved in the public affairs of society. It thinks about what is of general concern in the light of hope in Christ for the Kingdom of God. It becomes political in the name of the poor and marginalized in a given society. Remembrance of the Crucified Christ makes it critical toward political religions and idolatries. It thinks critically about the religious and moral values of societies in which it exists, and presents its reflections as a reasoned position.[7]

The Canadian churches' work on peace and disarmament provides an example of the possibilities of an effective public theology. Project Ploughshares, a highly respected peace project of the Canadian Council of Churches, has facilitated a *public theological* consensus between historic churches that had relied on a Christian just war tradition and the pacifist churches opposed to all use of force. Both traditions reached a uniquely Canadian theological accommodation whereby all churches agreed to a *policing role* for states in the broader framework of what Glenn Stassen would eventually describe as "just peacemaking."[8] In 2003, this consensus enabled 40,000 Canadians – 4,000 a week – to sign the public statement "Prepare for Peace in Iraq"[9] which Prime Minister Jean Chretien acknowledged helped keep Canada out of George W. Bush's illegal Iraq war.

Public ecumenism requires a *public theology* to support and inform its mission and work. In Canada, the term "public theology" is only beginning to be used. Nevertheless, since

---

7 Jürgen Moltmann, *God for a Secular Society: The Public Relevance of Theology*, trans. Margaret Kohl (Minneapolis: Fortress Press, 1999), 1.

8 Glen Harold Stassen, ed., *Just Peacemaking: Ten Practices for Abolishing War* (Cleveland, OH: Pilgrim Press, 1998).

9 "Project Ploughshares Accomplishments," Project Ploughshares: http://ploughshares.ca/about-us/accomplishments/. A public statement issued on January 17, 2003, by the Justice and Peace Commission of The Canadian Council of Churches, KAIROS: Canadian Ecumenical Justice Initiatives, and Project Ploughshares.

the Second World War, Canadian churches have embraced being public churches through an inclusive multifaith public ecumenism that has had an implicit public theology, which enabled them to contribute to Canada's public purpose.

BEING PUBLIC CHURCHES

Canadians are a winter people of diverse immigrant-settlers, who were welcomed by the First Nations to a vast and bountiful land. Together they created a country founded upon the idea of "peace, *welfare* and the good government,"[10] developing evolving narratives about who we are, what we do together, and our vision for the future. Churches, as one of the *custodians of the national identity,* helped shape Canadians' self-perception.

As the nation urbanized and industrialized, these newcomers needed schools, hospitals, community organizations, social services and a host of other institutions. Canadian churches understood their mission to help build a new country. The historian Mark Noll has noted that after Confederation in 1867, "Nation-building was the dominant theme in Canada's public life over that half century .... [Canadian churches] helped to shape Canada's emergence as a modern nation even as they were being shaped by it."[11] *Providing public services* to people and communities in need became an important contribution to humanize the Canadian project.

Public ecumenism's national interest continued as churches took on the mantle of being a *conscience for the nation,* putting

10 John Ralston Saul, *A Fair Country: Telling Truths about Canada* (Toronto: Penguin, 2009). Saul uses this early formulation of Canada's founding principle, which was later changed to the more familiar "peace, *order* and good government." This difference is important, because Saul's research reclaims the original idea of Canada with its Aboriginal or Indigenous origins as a nation. The term "winter people" is one I have often used to describe the hearty, steadfast, generous character of people who need each other to be Canadians in such a wonderful but unforgiving place.

11 Mark A. Noll, *A History of Christianity in the United States and Canada* (Grand Rapids, MI: Eerdmans, 1992), 250.

many important questions on the national and international agenda. This public role was foundational to establishing the Canadian Council of Churches in the late 1940s. During the 1970s and 1980s, it was embedded in the ecumenical cooperative spirit of the ecumenical coalitions that brought churches, religious orders and church development agencies together in common cause in working for justice, peace and integrity of creation.[12] It drove the Canadian Ecumenical Jubilee Initiative at the turn of the millennium and inspired the creation of KAIROS–Canadian Ecumenical Justice Initiatives that brought all these groups together into one of the pre-eminent education-advocacy organizations in the country.

With the disestablishment of Canadian churches, public ecumenism's caring for the national interest has once again transitioned into a role of *public accompaniment*. The Truth and Reconciliation Commission of Canada (TRC) was a watershed moment for Canada and for churches. Exposing the complicity of churches in Canada's colonial project of assimilation has been shattering and yet ironically, painfully cathartic. National Indigenous Anglican Bishop Mark MacDonald points out how in spite of the churches' complicity in "cultural genocide" that the TRC exposed, for churches it may be a moment of "grace" and "an opportunity to rediscover aspects of its foundational message and life that have been obscured by their long-term chaplaincy to Western society and its values and practices."[13]

---

12 D. Preman Niles, "Justice, Peace and the Integrity of Creation," World Council of Churches, *Ecumenical Dictionary – 2002 Revised Edition* (2003): http://www.wcc-coe.org/wcc/who/dictionary-article11.html. "The phrase 'justice, peace and the integrity of creation' (JPIC) is shorthand for a fuller statement: 'To engage member churches in a conciliar process of mutual commitment (covenant) to justice, peace and the integrity of creation should be a priority for World Council programmes.' Originally intended as a programme priority for the WCC by its Vancouver assembly (1983) and addressed to its member churches, it was subsequently expanded to include churches that are not members of the WCC, regional and national ecumenical organizations and all other movements committed to these issues."

13 Mark MacDonald, "What the TRC Reveals about the Churches," *Consensus* 37, no. 1 (2016): Article 6.

At the release of the TRC Report in June 2015, one of the Indigenous speakers said, "In all life, our purpose is accompanying others home."[14] In the wake of the shame and scandal of Residential Schools, public ecumenism has adopted a more humble and chastened role of public accompaniment of marginalized people and the vulnerable communities. Jennifer Henry of KAIROS has described this accompaniment with Indigenous peoples as "settler *ally-ship*."[15]

Public churches are drawn to the *public commons* in pursuit of the common good.[16] Such a pursuit requires understanding and discernment. Maria Cimperman argues that churches have "a sacred calling in the world" that can offer hope.[17] "[O]ur hope," Cimperman writes, "is rooted in God, it allows us to truly see the world as it is, to imagine more than what we see, and to work for what we sense is possible."[18] *Knowing* what is happening, *understanding* why it is happening and *acting* on what is happening are three important marks of public ecumenism.

I am always reminded how many Canadians, including people in the churches, are unaware of the significant contributions churches and particular church people have made to shaping Canada. This was brought home to me when my partner and I attended the State Dinner for Nelson Mandela at the Westin Harbour Castle in Toronto in June 1990. Mandela was released by South Africa in February of that year after more

14 The Release of the Report of the Truth and Reconciliation Commission of Canada, Ottawa, June 12, 2015.

15 Jennifer Henry, "Striving for Ethical Settler Allyship: Biblical Witness to Inspire," a workshop at *Reformation, Turmoil and Religious Experience: Tending Contemporary Expressions*, Renison University College, June 17, 2017.

16 David Pfrimmer, "Stewards of the Public Commons: A Vocation for Government and Church," in *Communion, Responsibility, Accountability: Responding as a Lutheran Communion to Neoliberal Globalization*, ed. Karen L. Bloomquist, LWF Documentation 50 (Geneva: Lutheran World Federation, 2004), 235–50.

17 Maria Cimperman, *Social Analysis for the 21st Century: How Faith Becomes Action* (Maryknoll, NY: Orbis Books, 2015), 1–25.

18 Ibid., 12.

than 27 years in prison. His first foreign trip was to Canada, to thank Canadians for their support in bringing an end to apartheid. What surprised me was how uninformed many of the dignitaries at our table were about the central role Canadian churches played in bringing an end to apartheid. But *Madiba* knew! The following morning, Mandela was thanking all the groups in what Haroon Siddiqui called "Nelson Mandela's Rainbow Coalition" of churches, labour unions and NGOs, those countless ordinary heroes, for their truly extraordinary support.

Whether as a custodian of the national identity, providing public services, serving as a conscience for the nation or publicly accompanying the vulnerable, public ecumenism's national purpose – even with its failings and complicity in injustice – was to care for people, for communities and, more recently, for creation itself. These public roles ensure that Canada might not just be a better place for Canadians, but would be a gift to the nations and a blessing to peoples and communities around the world.

PUBLIC MULTIFAITHISM FOR THE FUTURE

Ecumenism is changing because Canada and the world are changing. Our post-globalized, post-modern, post-colonial, post-truth, post-unitary world may be a place that requires a post-ecumenical movement. Just as with pastoral ecumenism, public ecumenism, too, may have reached its best-before date.

The paths forward and the possible paradigms are not clear in the midst of our fractured and at times conflicted public spaces. It will be an adventure. A post-ecumenical movement will need, as Kierkegaard suggested, to remember forward, probing and mining the wisdom and resources from our past. Such a movement will need to be inclusive, less theologically rigid, and organizationally more nimble, accepting a high degree of directional uncertainty. Such a movement I call *public multifaithism*.

Public multifaithism will begin its journey following at least three paths: (1) the disestablishment of Canadian churches, (2) Canada as a place of interfaith encounter, and (3) the emergence of new theological narrative(s) for global citizenship.

During the mid-1980s, Peter Newman argues that there was a Canadian Revolution whereby "The nation's defining institutions first lost their credibility, their authority, and finally their followers."[19] Douglas John Hall has described a similar experience of the churches as the "disestablishment of Christendom":

> The demise of Christendom is not just about the loss of numbers; it is about the loss of influence – including the influence of this faith among intellectual, artistic, and critical elites… Christians do not expect these elites to *endorse* the Christian faith, but they do hope that Christianity will be sufficiently stimulating to such representatives of "high culture" to be taken with some measure of seriousness. When Christianity is no longer noticed by critical elites, if only for purposes of argumentation… then it must be supposed that the process of disestablishment has run its full course.[20]

Public ecumenism always presumed to have a wider churched public that was sympathetic, was supportive and contributed to religious initiatives and institutions. Today, Canadians are not looking to religious leaders or organizations in the same way. However, disestablishment might have the silver lining of freeing the churches and other faith groups from the social and cultural expectations that compromise their message. Public multifaithism can mean greater freedom to be more provocative and prophetic in its justice seeking, peace building and ecological initiatives.

19 Peter C. Newman, *The Canadian Revolution, 1985–1995: From Deference to Defiance* (Toronto: Viking, 1995), 69.

20 Douglas John Hall, *The Cross in Our Context: Jesus and the Suffering World* (Minneapolis: Fortress Press, 2003), 161.

Successive generations of immigrants have each brought much to this country, including their faith. When they arrived, they encountered a rich and complex religious reality. Often unacknowledged Indigenous spirituality and values were embedded within Canada's culture and institutions. For many Indigenous peoples, spirituality has been embedded in their resistance to colonization and assimilation. More recently, Indigenous spirituality is being recognized and given a respected public place.[21] All this has made Canada a somewhat unique place where many varied and different faiths have encountered each other.

There have certainly been stumbles, missteps and mistakes in the past. Racism is still a reality in Canada. Religious prejudice and tension have played out in our history. Nevertheless, churches eventually learned to respect, understand, cooperate and collaborate with other faith traditions. This dynamic is being repeated today with more recently arrived faith communities. While there are bursts of religious and racial intolerance, these have been met more often than not with even stronger efforts to counter the purveyors of hatred and bigotry.

Bibby points out that "things are anything but over for religion in Canada," but they will be different from the past.[22] Bibby also argues that people of faith will need to "cross bridges" and "religious group boundaries" to build "denominational and interfaith ministerials, councils and ministry initiatives."[23] He notes that "As religious groups and religious organizations locate themselves and redefine themselves in a religiously polarized Canada, we can expect some infrastructures will

21 Indigenous spirituality is complex and is not a faith or religion per se. It represents more a worldview or a way of life. It is mentioned here only to acknowledge its roles in the Canadian religious landscape. As the Ontario Human Rights Commission has rightly pointed out, "The OHRC does not define 'Indigenous Spirituality' in recognition of its diversity and Indigenous peoples' right to define and determine this for themselves."

22 Bibby, *A New Day*.

23 Ibid., 39–40.

need to be created and many older infrastructures revised. Some will disappear."[24] As a "meeting place" of various faiths and spiritualities, Canada may yet provide a creative theological laboratory for the development of specific instances and institutions of public multifaithism.

Public ecumenism relied on an embedded theological narrative – The Dominion of Canada as a Christian nation – to provide a public ethical imperative for social action and solidarity. Public multifaithism will need to develop new, more nuanced theological narrative(s) to inspire and guide its concern for the care of Canada. Disestablished churches will need to self-critically interrogate their previous theological narratives and histories. Recently arrived faith traditions that have brought their theological narratives from away will now need to examine their own assumptions and practices. This can be painful and unsettling. Many ethnic churches that came previously with waves of immigration had to undergo the same soul searching.

Amid a culture of disbelief, where faith is either treated like a personal hobby or seen as the problem, there is a crisis of meaning for many people. Bibby makes the point that many Canadians are looking to have their spiritual, personal and relational needs met. They are not necessarily looking for greater public engagement. For public multifaithism to gain attention and support, it will be necessary to articulate compelling theological narratives that provide people with meaning, purpose and vision for their lives. Without such narratives, public multifaithism might at best merely resemble the good work of many other non-governmental organizations.

WHAT DOES PUBLIC MULTIFAITHISM REQUIRE?

Looking back over the past seven decades of the ecumenical movement, Canadian churches have made an important

24 Ibid., 47.

contribution to caring for Canada. These churches have not always fulfilled their public role in noble and exemplary ways, but they have endeavoured to try to be faithful public churches serving the common good. New winds of expectation are blowing across Canada. Some are troublesome. Some are refreshing. Some are hopeful, and some are just plain long overdue. What insights from our ecumenical past offer some wisdom and direction?

Public multifaithism will require *confessional acuity*. Multifaithism does not mean minimizing your own faith tradition. It does mean you need to be theologically literate to articulate your own tradition as an effective multifaith partner. Christians will need to be fully Christian in order for Muslims or Jews or others to be fully faithful to their own tradition in these encounters. This is a different approach than authoritatively and dogmatically asserting our truth against all others. In fact, it is what many churches and faith communities are already doing.

Public multifaithism will require *border crossing* by the faithful. Jesus was the master adventure guide. He took his disciples on risky field trips where no self-respecting Jews in his day would go. Public multifaithism will need just such adventure guides – leaders willing to risk taking their people and communities beyond the places, experiences and practices of their own comfortable worlds.

With increasing polarizing and fragmenting of civic life, public multifaithism will require patience and persistence in *convening publics*. *Publics* are those voluntary associations of individuals who are changed as they come together around an idea or cause and in turn change their communities and their world. Convening such publics will require professionalism, competency and commitment to community organizing practices.

Public multifaithism will require collective discernment and wisdom to *name the public questions.* It is not enough just to address a question in the limited terms of how it impacts my faith community. Public multifaithism requires the ethical and theological abilities to analyze, discern, understand and articulate a public question that resonates with and speaks to hearts and minds of a wider public. It will depend on social-political intelligence to responsibly participate in the public commons with a host of other actors seeking the common good.

Public multifaithism is about engagement with God's world and offering people a confident and meaningful worldview to understand why the world is the way it is and what people of faith can do about it. Public multifaithism changes the faith communities themselves just as they come together to change the world. A number of years ago, there was a billboard that read, "Don't make me come down there! God." Public multifaithism will help the world see that She is already here!

David Pfrimmer is professor of Public Ethics and co-director of the Centre for Public Ethics at Waterloo Lutheran Seminary on the campus of Wilfrid Laurier University in Waterloo, Ontario. He is also an International Fellow at the Chester Ronning Centre for the Study of Religion and Public Life at the University of Alberta. He has chaired the Canadian Council of Churches' Commission for Justice and Peace and served on several boards of ecumenical coalitions for social justice.

LIVING INTO THE LINEAGE OF JUSTICE-SEEKING CHRISTIANS IN CANADA

Photo by Gerald Deo

CHRISTINE BOYLE

The day of my final interview to be approved for ordination, January 20, 2017, was the day that Donald Trump was inaugurated President of the United States. The overlap of these events weighed on me.

I like to believe in progress. I like to believe the line that Dr. Martin Luther King famously quoted from theologian Theodore Parker: "the moral arc of the universe is long, but it bends toward justice." On January 20, I was deeply agnostic about progress.

To be a young woman, a parent of young kids, and called into ordered ministry is at the best of times a bit daunting. And these are far from the best of times.

The evening before that final interview, I sat around an old dining room table among leafy salads and Japanese dumplings, in the company of two dear women friends. Both are dedicated community workers, passionate feminists, spiritual seekers and exhausted parents. Between the three of us we have six kids. As we opened the floodgates of our anxiety and lament about the state of the world, the five youngest kids ran and crawled and chased in circles around us… layers of chaos, speckled with the kids' squeals of delight.

The following day was the Women's March on Washington and solidarity marches around the globe. I was at the Vancouver march, toddler in tow, along with more than 30 members of my congregation. The previous evening's conversation had convinced me I needed to be surrounded by people whose presence could remind me that not everything had changed. I needed the physical presence of others to remind me that there was still love and solidarity in the world, resistance in the face of this latest expression of hate and greed.

Reading the reflections in this book has served a similar purpose for me. They have kept me company. They have reminded me of the lineage of Christian activism I endeavour to be part of. They have surrounded my despair and forced it to surrender.

I could write pages about my gratitude to those who have been doing this work for far longer than I have been alive. The stories in this book rightly testify to their presence and persistence. Some of the folks in these stories have mentored and encouraged me, some are strangers whose efforts I hear spoken about time and again, and many are stories I might never have encountered, but whose impacts I am fortunate to live in. I feel indebted to them all. There is huge value in the sort of education that telling and retelling these stories provides, across generations. My gratitude runs deep.

But just as I cringe at being referred to as "the future" of the church, I don't want to simply eulogize the church of our past. Many of the great leaders spoken of in these chapters are still fighting the good fight today. There is still work to be done. It is work that the gospel clearly calls us to, that Jesus set a clear example of, that God is present in.

Let us draw strength from the stories of our past, and learn lessons from them about how people of faith can be active and effective leaders in co-creating a more just and loving world.

LESSON #1: A BIGGER SENSE OF WHAT IS POSSIBLE

When organizing among secular folks of my generation, I am frequently struck by their passion and conviction, and by the hurried timeframe we have grown accustomed to. In a 24-hour news cycle, and a world of very short-term memory, people of faith bring a longer time frame, a deeper perspective.

Christians come from ancient stories. Stories that are older than this electoral system, older than this economic system. We come from stories that remind us that all sorts of miraculous transformations are possible. When we forget this, when we don't learn our history, change feels impossible, because it feels like things have always been just as they are now.

The stories of our traditions remind us that a better way is possible. A more trusting way of relating to one another. A fairer way of organizing our lives and our resources. And most importantly, a more inspiring and purposeful way of understanding and measuring success – reframing what a good life looks like.

Pope Francis' 2015 encyclical *Laudato Si'* touches eloquently on this challenge. So did the Catholic bishops' 1983 statement "Ethical Reflections on the Economic Crisis." Both embrace a longer, larger view of what is possible, naming what is needed and urgent right now.

Christians, the bearers of dangerous memory, are people who know a truth larger than the free market, more compelling than austerity, more rewarding than individualism.

In his chapter, David Pfrimmer speaks about early ecumenical cooperation to develop a faith-based response to free trade. He notes that churches didn't just oppose, but they proposed an alternative economic vision and economics of enough where all people and communities mattered.

It made me think about the Leap Manifesto. Initiated and launched in 2015, the Leap Manifesto is "a plan for how Canada can move to a clean energy economy in a way that addresses systemic racism and economic inequality."[1] Many political pundits and media outlets immediately wrote it off as too radical. Rex Murphy called it "a wild-eyed, ultra-greenist, anti-capitalist dogma-sheet."

What makes the Leap so radical? It calls for a Canada based on caring for the earth and one another. It states that "public scarcity in times of unprecedented private wealth is a manufactured crisis, designed to extinguish our dreams before they have a chance to be born." And it names "our sacred duty to those this country harmed in the past, to those suffering needlessly in the present, and to all who have a right to a bright and safe future."

Its initiating signatories include National Indigenous Anglican Bishop Mark MacDonald, Jesuit priests Jean-Marc Biron and Peter Bisson, Citizens for Public Justice, KAIROS, and an abundance of secular creative and social movement leaders.

Signatories were acting as bearers of dangerous memory, with the courage and creativity to reimagine our future in light

1 https://theleap.org/faqs/

of a long and storied past. It's one of the most valuable gifts that people of faith continue to offer. We see things both old and new, and are part of living into new stories, new possibilities, repeatedly.

LESSON #2: THE OPPORTUNITY INHERENT IN OUR DEMISE

The church that I was raised in, that imbued a sense of purpose in me as a teenager, that called me into leadership as a young adult, wasn't a church of Christendom. The church that I fell in love with, the theology that pulled at me, the God and the incarnate Christ that I knew from my earliest days have always been counter-cultural.

Today's church has little illusion of power. Not because we are inherently humble and Christ-like, but because our numbers have shrunk rapidly enough to force humility upon us. And while I, like many, grieve the shrinking numbers, I am nonetheless optimistic about what we will learn in this next incarnation of our life as church.

The church of Christendom was a colonizing (and, my peers might say, a "mansplaining") church. It participated in cultural and human genocide, wiping out rich ways of knowing and practising faith in God. It assumed it knew better than everyone else, creating strict hierarchies and embedding competition, isolation and secrecy into each level. It lost my generation not because the music was too quiet but because the hypocrisy was too loud.

We have less mainstream influence and social credibility than we once had. So the tactics that were effective 50 years ago aren't necessarily going to have an impact now.

In his reflection, Tony Clarke talks about the value of participatory democracy, and how the bishops' pastoral methodology delivered a powerful moral message. A methodology of listening to their congregants, and providing leadership that reflected their needs. Sr. Marie Zarowny's work on family violence in the North outlines a similar approach. It's a methodology that Jesus' own ministry seems to have followed.

There is a possibility for deep and participatory engagement in faith communities. A possibility for transformative conversation, and the building of relationships across lines of class, age and race. A possibility for leaders to amplify the voices of their community, speaking to issues that touch those outside the community. As Clarke says, "'Ethical Reflections' touched people who were outcasts due to the policies of that time."

When we were powerful, our leaders met with prime ministers, and our steeples defined landscapes. But often when we're more powerful, we're less willing to rock the boat. After all, we've got a comfortable seat aboard. The opportunity of decline is in realigning ourselves with those on the sidelines, taking more risks and being less worried about the privilege we might lose in doing so.

LESSON #3: A TIME FOR MULTI-FAITH COLLABORATION

For decades, we have challenged ourselves to work ecumenically, and have felt proud of ourselves for our ability to look beyond differences in liturgy or hierarchy or soteriology in order to work together on issues of common cause. Ecumenical work is important, slow, tedious and frustrating. I have great respect for those who are doing it. I also know that, in a deeply and imperfectly multicultural, post-Christian country, it just isn't enough.

Effective justice and advocacy work requires an ability to reach and mobilize sufficiently large numbers of people, and an ability to use social license to shift the frame of what is both viable and valuable. The death of Christendom, the loss of public credibility, and the changing demographics of Canada mean that to have large impact, our faith-based justice work must become multi-faith.

This has started to happen in churches and ecumenical coalitions reaching out to form relationships and act in solidarity with local Indigenous communities and organizations. These relationships are vitally important for our own healing, since our history is interwoven with the horrors of colonization and our central role in Residential Schools.

Bill Phipps talks about the period of introspection that the United Church went through in the decade that preceded his time as Moderator. He then led efforts to wean the church from a focus on charity to a prioritizing of justice. The shift from ecumenical to multi-faith collaboration is a similar widening of the lens – possible because of the respectful ecumenical conversations and collaborations that have taken place. Now it is time to broaden our sights again.

I don't mean the sort of multi-faith events where a panel of religious leaders (usually white men) share something charming and unique about their tradition, and then everyone goes home feeling lukewarm: "Isn't it great that we all basically believe in the same God." We've done that.

Building relationships through shared meals, and through experiencing one another's rituals and holidays, isn't enough. We need to sink into our differences and form relationships of solidarity despite those differences, rather than friendships that glaze over them. Are we willing to defend one another and to stand together in common cause on the issues that our faiths call us to speak for?

We can't leave this work on an individual, ad hoc basis. We need structures and coordinated coalitions that help move it forward, and amplify the impact. I often hear from discouraged pastors who say, "My congregation put out a great statement about X, Y or Z, but no one noticed." Our actions and commentary receive less media coverage and attract less attention than decades ago. To mobilize more people, we must build larger platforms from which to challenge the status quo.

It's worth looking for inspiration to the Moral Mondays movement in the United States. This new multi-ethnic, multi-religious coalition, with an anti-racist, anti-poverty agenda, has been mobilizing mass numbers of people and regularly engaging in nonviolent civil disobedience. The movement has spread across the southern US, drawing on the history and religious stories and values of supporters.

At this moment in Canadian history, Christian churches hold enough social weight that we can't shy away from speaking on issues of concern, but not enough weight that we can assume simply raising our voices will be sufficient. We need allies, and our allies need us.

LESSON #4: LEADERSHIP IN THESE TIMES

The challenge of stretching from individual to ecumenical to multi-faith highlights what I think is the largest challenge we face: the need for leaders who are ready and trained to rise to the task.

In this book, several names come up again and again. Bold and creative leaders, willing to take risks. None of the important shifts in the history of this country, from peacekeeping to health care to enfranchisement for women and marginalized communities, have happened easily. These efforts have required great leaders, coordinated coalitions and tireless work. And they will continue to need these.

John Olthuis says, "You don't have many visionary Social Gospel politicians like Tommy Douglas around these days...." Do we have fewer bold public leaders as our churches shrink? Or does it always seem to young people that past generations had more courageous leaders? How can we become those leaders?

I have been incredibly fortunate in the mentoring and support I have received. I feel so fortunate because I see how uncommon that intergenerational support is for my peers.

Historically, one of the Christian church's great contributions to a just and peaceful society has been in its raising and training of new generations who understand their role in strengthening that social fabric. In Canada we, alongside the labour movement, have played central roles in developing lifelong leaders able to effectively advocate for the public good. Being an intergenerational community, we haven't needed to be specific and strategic about succession. However, in decline, both churches and the labour movement aren't turning out the quality and quantity of leaders they once did.

It's not that those people no longer exist. It's that we don't know who they are, and they don't trust who we are. So, all the powerful and radical leadership curricula we create aren't reaching the people who might hunger for and benefit from them. Faith and spirituality continue to be seen as private, personal matters to younger generations.

We have the skills, wisdom, elders – and, in some places, the funding – to close that gap. Young people today aren't any less spiritually inclined than in the past. They are, in fact, just as mindful, smart, passionate and thoughtful as previous generations who were once young, too.

Models exist, such as the Next Up Leadership Program. It's an eight-month leadership program for young people committed to environmental and social justice. Launched in BC in 2006, it now runs in seven Canadian cities. Next Up also offers multi-day intensives, focusing on supporting young Indigenous leaders. The program seeks out young people already engaging in justice work, and trains and supports them to strengthen that work, to build intergenerational and cross-sector relationships. Each year there are hundreds more applicants than there are spaces.

At the Victoria, BC, Pride parade this year, Rev. Michelle Slater wore her collar underneath a t-shirt that read, "Hurt by church? Get a str8 apology here." I am a straight, cis-gendered woman, but I wept when I read that, because more and more examples of humble, courageous faith leaders in the public sphere are needed.

LESSON #5: MY OWN LEARNING ON CLIMATE JUSTICE

I was late to climate justice. When I started getting involved in climate activism, the science was already alarming. We were decades behind where we needed to be in terms of transitioning to a green economy. Very little action was being taken.

The end of 2012 was nearly seven years into the regime of Stephen Harper's Conservatives. The likelihood of timely and science-based climate action in Canada was then at an all-time low. I have an aversion to conflict and confrontation, but I collaborated with a handful of folks to create Fossil Free Faith: Canada's Interfaith Divestment Network. I leaned into where I found hope, and I spent the better part of the last five years – through the loss of a baby, and then the birth of a son, theological school, maternity leave, family illness and more – living and breathing divestment and climate action. I travelled to the Vatican for the release of *Laudato Si'*, and I went to Paris for COP21. But mostly I had lots of conversations, sent lots of emails, preached, witnessed and showed up to listen.

Frequently, I received encouragement among friends and colleagues in faith-based justice circles. Equally often, I received patronizing explanations of what, it was assumed, I clearly didn't understand. I was told that divestment was too negative, or divisive, and that shareholder engagement was working just fine. I wrestled with a leader in my denomination about differences of opinion on civil disobedience and when it might be the right kind of trouble. Those years of fossil fuel divestment advocacy shaped me, and left me with a few wounds.

Moira Hutchinson writes that shareholder engagement, not divestment, made the difference in South Africa (though most retellings of the anti-apartheid movement acknowledge that these efforts all played a role). Strategically, when and how do we decide if shareholder engagement is still working, and if it is working fast enough? Divestment does not mean we walk away from the issue. Most of the people working on divestment (from fossil fuels, or in mining justice, or for a just peace in Palestine) are also working hard on those challenges from a variety of other angles.

More personally, the debate brings up intergenerational questions of expertise and of urgency. It is likely that shareholder engagement on climate justice requires more patience than I have, and more time than the climate science tells us we have. How are we responding to the passion and impatience of our young leaders and to the real fear and urgency that people are experiencing?

It's true that our ancient stories bring a longer timeframe to social movement work. It's also true that there are challenges that require us to move faster than our institutions are designed to move. I wrestle with this tension. Sometimes the church feels like a soothing balm for the parts of me that are on fire. And sometimes it feels like our whole building is on fire, and we are standing inside, singing dirge-like hymns.

A FAITH THAT LOOKS LIKE THE WOMEN'S MARCH ON WASHINGTON

The United Church of Canada's New (1968) Creed begins and ends with the line "We are not alone." It's the most concise summary of my own theology. That, and this line from the Apostles' Creed: "I believe in the communion of saints."

My faith is nurtured in chaotic, inspiring dinners among friends and strangers and loud children. At its best, my faith looks like the Women's March on Washington. It looks like the weaving together of gospel and politics and presence in community. That's where I am most in touch with God, most authentically living into my calling. And it's fed, fuelled, challenged, refined and strengthened by relationships inside and outside the church.

My hope lies in the possibility that this work might first reinvigorate us. Engaging with those doing justice work outside of our small and shrinking circles, we might see, hear and feel the gospel anew, through the lives of those who are doing it with the passion of the one we seek to follow. In fiery young people, in justice-seeking leaders of other faiths, in fishers, and taxi drivers, and hospital cleaning staff. Listening to their stories might get us off our high horse, and re-enliven us for the real and gritty work of turning this world around.

Lest I not get too comfortable myself, I remind myself of a prayer crafted by Colin Winter, an Anglican bishop who was expelled from Namibia for his opposition to apartheid: "Lord, remind me when I need to know, You did not ask me to defend your Church but to lay down my life for people."[2]

Rev. Christine Boyle was raised on unceded Coast Salish territory in Vancouver, BC. She has a B.Sc. in Urban Agriculture and First Nations Studies from UBC, and an M.A. in Religious Leadership for Social Change from the Graduate Theological Union in Berkeley, California.

She has done community outreach and anti-poverty advocacy in the Downtown Eastside, and supported the development of GreenJobs BC. Christine launched Spirited Social Change, initiated The Self Care Project, and co-created Fossil Free Faith: Canada's Interfaith Divestment Network.

In January 2016, Christine joined the team at Canadian Memorial United Church and Centre for Peace as Minister of Community Life. She is also on the Board of the United Church Observer. *She has a teenage stepdaughter and a three-year-old son.*

2 Mending the World (1997). United Church of Canada: http://www.united-church.ca/sites/default/files/resources/report_mending-the-world.pdf.

LET'S LOOK UPSTREAM TO DO JUSTICE

Photo by Katia Taylor

LEAH WATKISS

The stories and struggles described in this book were enlightening and inspirational. I hadn't previously appreciated the extent to which the Christian churches have influenced and shaped this country. It was wonderful to read stories of Christians on the frontline of justice work in the 1970s and '80s. I'm grateful to Joe for taking the time to record these stories and hope they will be shared widely. But while I understand these stories to be part of a legacy of Christian justice work, I didn't experience any of them, and they are not part of my generation's collective memory.

I am a millennial, born in the 1980s. In my lifetime, the issues that Christian churches have been most consistently vocal about are abortion, contraception, LGBTQ+ rights, euthanasia and assisted dying. At the moment, the legacy of the Christian church in Canada is dominated by discussion of Residential Schools, and every few months a new story of sexual abuse by Catholic clergy emerges. The church is seen by many of my generation as outdated, conservative and oppressive.

With this legacy, it's little wonder that so many of my friends have turned away from the church. I have attended lots of weddings, but only a handful have taken place in churches. And although I have been to many baby showers, few of them have been followed up with baptisms.

Fortunately for me, I was raised by feminist Catholics who had their coming of age during Vatican II. By their words and actions, they instilled in me the understanding that social justice, peace and ecological work is fundamental to being Christian. They also taught me about informed conscience. I'm grateful for those teachings, because I didn't learn them from attending church or from Catholic school. My parents immigrated to Canada after most of the movements outlined in this book, but they hold and passed on to me a vision of church that is rooted in love and compassion for those who are oppressed and marginalized.

This vision of church and Christianity has now become mainstream thanks to the election of Pope Francis. Under him, we have had a resurgence of interest in Catholic Social Teaching. Although the moral teachings haven't changed, Pope Francis has shifted the tone of the conversation and has demonstrated openness to dialogue. His integral ecology encyclical, *Laudato Si'*, has made its mark in both religious and secular realms.

Those of us who have been doing justice and ecology work find ourselves torn sometimes between our delight in Pope

Francis' resurrection of social justice work and our exasperation with those who think that this is a radical new direction for the church. Whether or not people appreciate the legacy upon which Pope Francis' work is built (which has biblical roots and whose modern movement dates back to the 19th century), it is wonderful to have Catholicism and Christianity associated once again with justice work. But as easy as it is to get swept up in the Francis effect and to pat ourselves on the back for a job well done, Christian churches still tend to approach justice work with the mindset of doing *for*, not doing *with*.

This approach is reflected well in a story I heard at a faith-based anti-poverty gathering a few years ago. As part of the introduction to the day, one of the organizers told us about a fictional picnic by a river that he felt embodied the justice work we were all there to pursue. The story went like this:

> There's a church picnic by the river. The churchgoers notice somebody drowning, so they fish that person out and rescue them. Shortly after, they notice another person drowning. They rescue that person, too. Then they notice another person, and another, and another. They set up a net across the river to catch all the people who are coming down the river drowning. They pat themselves on the back for a job well done of rescuing drowning people.
>
> Finally, someone in the group says: let's go find out why all these people are ending up drowning. Upon investigation, they find a broken bridge. They decide to fix the bridge to stop people from falling into the river and drowning in the first place.

This story is a great metaphor for the kind of charity and justice work that most Christians engage in. They recognize a problem in which others are suffering, identify a way to respond to the immediate problem (charity), and then set out to fix the problem (justice).

However, there are several significant problems with this metaphor that reflect an oppressive and paternalistic approach to justice work that I outline below.

Saviour Complex: In both halves of this story, the rescuers are depicted as the saviours of people in need who are passive recipients and cannot help themselves. This portrayal denies the autonomy, ingenuity and prerogative of people who are oppressed to achieve their own liberation.

Culpability of the Rescuers: The privileged rescuers of this story appear to exist outside of the problem and aren't aware of the role they play in the reason people are drowning. In reality, there is always a link between privilege and oppression. Advantages based on things like wealth, gender and race are experienced by some because disadvantages are experienced by others based on those same factors. White privilege, for example, exists because people of colour are oppressed. Engaging in real justice work requires us to acknowledge that our privilege comes at the expense of the oppression of others.

Voiceless Victim: In this story, the people being rescued have no voice. There is no indication that the drowning victims are given room to say anything. When the rescuers decide that they are interested in what's happening upstream, they go up to investigate. In fact, they should be asking the people they pull out of the river, "What happened? How did you end up here?" The answer would reveal a bigger picture of social problems and might point to a different solution.

Victim Blaming: When you read this story, while congratulating the clever rescuers for how ingenious they are for fixing the bridge, part of you is thinking the whole time, "Why would someone walk across a broken bridge? Those people should have known better."

I've just scratched the surface here; it's evident that there are a lot of problems that need to be reconsidered with this approach to justice.

In nonviolence work, it is said that "means are ends in the making." In other words, when you pursue a goal, the end result will be a direct result of the means used to achieve it. Therefore, when we use violence to achieve peace, we are perpetuating violent systems and institutions. The resulting "peace" will be one of conflict and violence.

This principle applies equally to justice work. When we work for justice operating with biases and assumptions and within institutions that are sexist, racist, homophobic, ableist and prejudiced in other ways, the results we achieve will continue to exist within those types of structures.

The clearest example of the dangers of using ends to justify means is that of Indian Residential Schools. Privileged white Christians decided that they knew what was best for the Indigenous peoples of Canada, and employed brutal, often horrific means of achieving that goal. They justified their acts as being in the best interests of a group they thought couldn't take care of or speak for themselves. The result was devastating. Over 150,000 children were ripped from their families; over 6,000 died. There have been more than 32,000 claims of sexual assault taking place in the schools. The intergenerational impacts include poor health, poor education, the loss of Indigenous languages and culture, and addictions and suicides. The schools are all closed now; with the completion of the Truth and Reconciliation Commission, settlers would like to think that this chapter of Canadian history has been closed, too. But that basic framework is still operating in our society and in our churches.

One of the ways we see this framework alive and well is in our language. Many of us doing justice work talk about "the poor," "the homeless," "the alienated," and "being a voice for the voiceless." These terms are paternalistic and derogatory. They propagate the notion that those who are oppressed are a homogenous, separate "other" group of society who can't speak for themselves and need rescuing. If we are operating within those biases and assumptions, any progress we might make on that front is inherently still oppressive. We may improve the lives and situations of those who are marginalized, but the result still objectifies a group of people and strips them of their dignity. We may end up doing more harm than good.

I have seen this dynamic play out in the anti-human trafficking work I do. Human trafficking is an abhorrent crime where people are forced, through violence, deception and/or coercion, into activities for the purpose of exploitation. It includes, but is not limited to, forced labour, sexual exploitation, forced street crime and domestic servitude.

Today's anti-trafficking movement has its roots in the late 19th-century anti-white slavery movement that fought the procurement of white women and girls for forced sex work. This framework placed ultimate value on the sexual purity of white women and focused on rescuing victims and putting criminals behind bars.

Many anti-trafficking groups, especially faith-based ones, operate from this framework today. Because it serves the interests of the "rescuers" and fails to consider the root causes of the problem, it has had little success in lessening incidences of trafficking. In fact, it has been known to result in policies that actually make trafficking worse. That is why when Faith Alliance to End Human Trafficking (Faith Alliance) was formed, we knew that we wanted to do this work differently.

Faith Alliance is a collaboration of religious and other partners working to end human trafficking by raising awareness and inspiring action. It is operated by the Sisters of St. Joseph of Toronto. In 2015, during the Pan and Parapan Am Games, Faith Alliance undertook a public education and awareness campaign called GIFT Box in collaboration with the UN Global Initiative to Fight Trafficking (UN.GIFT) and STOP THE TRAFFIK. GIFT Box is a walk-in piece of public art that invites passers-by inside with the kinds of promises and offers that traffickers use to lure people. Once inside, visitors are presented with the realities of human trafficking.

Faith Alliance decided to bring GIFT Box to Canada to provide a snapshot of the lives of real people who have been trafficked in the Toronto area, giving a human face and voice to some of the 30 million people worldwide who have experienced human trafficking.

Coming together to embark on this project, Faith Alliance decided to adopt the anti-oppression framework that had been recently created by the Toronto Counter Human Trafficking Network (operated by the FCJ Refugee Centre). As a group comprised largely of privileged people, formally committing to working from an anti-oppression framework forced us to ask different questions and make decisions that were not instinctual for us.

One difficult decision we faced was how to approach the legality of sex work. The dominant anti-trafficking movement has a focus on sexual purity. This perspective is biased in its approach to sex work, viewing all sex work as morally wrong, and considers all sex workers to be victims unable to consent to their work. However, not all sex work is done through coercion. Conflating sex work and sex trafficking is harmful. Broadly speaking, the spectrum of people engaged in sex work includes those there because of choice, circumstance and coercion. When you look at sex work from an anti-oppressive framework, you prioritize the voices of those with lived experience. Instead of falling back on your own bias, you ask questions and listen to the answers. So we sought out the voice of sex workers on human trafficking and sexual exploitation. We heard from them that pushing for the criminalization of sex work, whether through prosecution of the sex workers (the traditional approach) or through the prosecution of those who purchase sex (what has become known as "the Nordic Model"), puts sex workers across the spectrum in greater danger of abuse and exploitation, and makes it harder for them to report instances of exploitation. Consequently, Faith Alliance agreed not to push for criminalization. Instead, we agreed to acknowledge that sex work has a spectrum and to advocate for policies that make it easier for sex workers to access supports and report instances of exploitation.

This decision was not easy, but it proved to be the right one. Over the course of the Pan and Parapan Am Games, we had several sex workers approach our volunteers at the GIFT Box to ask about our stance and explain how anti-trafficking work makes their jobs harder and more dangerous. As our anti-oppression approach had been part of our volunteer training and orientation, our volunteers had productive conversations with the sex workers. They left satisfied that they had been heard and that although we didn't promote sex work, we were not engaging in tactics or approaches that would put them at greater risk. Volunteers were able to explain and convey this message to the over 1,200 people who experienced GIFT Box, and to their churches and organizations as well.

Moving forward, Faith Alliance continues to have difficult conversations and to critique our work in accordance with our anti-oppression framework. By no means have we perfected our anti-oppression approach: it's an ongoing process of learning and discernment. We sometimes slip back into the language of victimhood, or make paternalistic assumptions about people who have been trafficked. But by surrounding our organization with other like-minded people and groups, we hold each other accountable.

My experience with Faith Alliance taught me that Christians who want to engage in real justice work should periodically ask a few important questions. The first is this: Why do we want to do this work? Feeling good, although undoubtedly a by-product of being a part of the justice movement, is not in itself the right answer. If we are primarily motivated by self-interest, our actions and decisions will serve only ourselves. Instead, our motivation should come from a place of solidarity: from the recognition that all of God's creation deserves to flourish and thrive.

The second question is this: Whose voices are being heard? Answering this question requires us to pay attention to more than who is in the room; we must pay attention to the ways that systems of oppression privilege certain voices over others. Even if they are present, people who belong to marginalized and oppressed groups often have trouble making themselves heard. If they do not feel that they are in a safe space, they may choose not to speak. If they do speak up, their contributions may not be taken as seriously. In my work with Christians, I generally find that men take up most of the speaking time, even when they are a small proportion of those in attendance. It's important for our structures to ensure that the voices of those affected by our work be heard. This includes the voices of those we are trying to help directly, and those who could be impacted indirectly from our work. For example, in human trafficking work, it's important to hear the voices of those who have been trafficked as well as migrant workers, sex workers and others.

The third question is this: Is our movement accessible, or are there barriers that would prevent people from participating based on their gender, sexual orientation, race, poverty, ability or any other factor? Providing things like free childcare and transit tokens for those who attend, and choosing locations that are wheelchair and transit accessible, are examples of ways we can reduce barriers and bring a diversity of people and voices into our movements.

The fourth question is this: Does our work challenge power structures and systems of oppression that perpetuate injustice? This question goes back to our river story. Are we rescuing the people who are drowning by taking it upon ourselves to fix a bridge? Or are we asking questions and coming up with solutions to change the whole system of privilege and oppression that created the problem in the first place? Answering these questions might involve taking a long, hard look in the mirror at the ways that our privilege comes at the expense of others, but this self-examination is the root of liberation.

An Aboriginal activist group in Queensland came up with this phrase in the 1970s: "If you have come here to help me you are wasting your time, but if you have come because your liberation is bound up with mine, then let us work together."[1] Christians need to root our justice work in this framework of solidarity. Only then will we truly start building the kingdom of God.

Leah Watkiss holds a master's degree in Peace and Justice from the University of San Diego, where she worked as the graduate assistant for Catholic Social Thought and completed a mentorship program in applied nonviolence. She has done peace and justice work for several Christian organizations, including Pace e Bene Nonviolence Services, the Anglican Diocese of Toronto and Citizens for Public Justice. Leah serves as program director of the Ministry for Social Justice, Peace, and Care of Earth with the Sisters of St. Joseph of Toronto.

1 Note: this quote is often attributed to Lilla Watson, but she has stated that it was the result of a collective process and prefers it be attributed as such.

FSC
www.fsc.org
RECYCLED
Paper made from recycled material
FSC® C103567

Printed on Rolland Enviro, which contains 100% post-consumer fiber, is ECOLOGO, Processed Chlorine Free, Ancient Forest Friendly and FSC® certified and is manufactured using renewable biogas energy.

PERMANENT 100% BIO GAS® ENERGY Ancient Forest Friendly™